A History of the Company
of Pikemen and Musketeers

A History of the Company of Pikemen and Musketeers

Richard Frase

First published in Great Britain in 2026 by
Pen & Sword History
An imprint of Pen & Sword Books Limited
Yorkshire – Philadelphia

ISBN 978 1 03614 233 9

A CIP catalogue record for this book is
available from the British Library.

Typeset by Mac Style
Printed in the UK by CPI Group (UK) Ltd, Croydon, CR0 4YY.

The Publisher's authorised representative in the EU for product
safety is Authorised Rep Compliance Ltd., Ground Floor,
71 Lower Baggot Street, Dublin D02 P593, Ireland.
www.arccompliance.com

For a complete list of Pen & Sword titles please contact:

PEN & SWORD BOOKS LIMITED
47 Church Street, Barnsley, South Yorkshire, S70 2AS, England
E-mail: enquiries@pen-and-sword.co.uk
Website: www.pen-and-sword.co.uk
or
PEN AND SWORD BOOKS
1950 Lawrence Road, Havertown, PA 19083, USA
E-mail: uspen-and-sword@casematepublishers.com
Website: www.penandswordbooks.com

Contents

Appendices

to Cassian

ROUTE OF THE LORD MAYOR'S SHOW

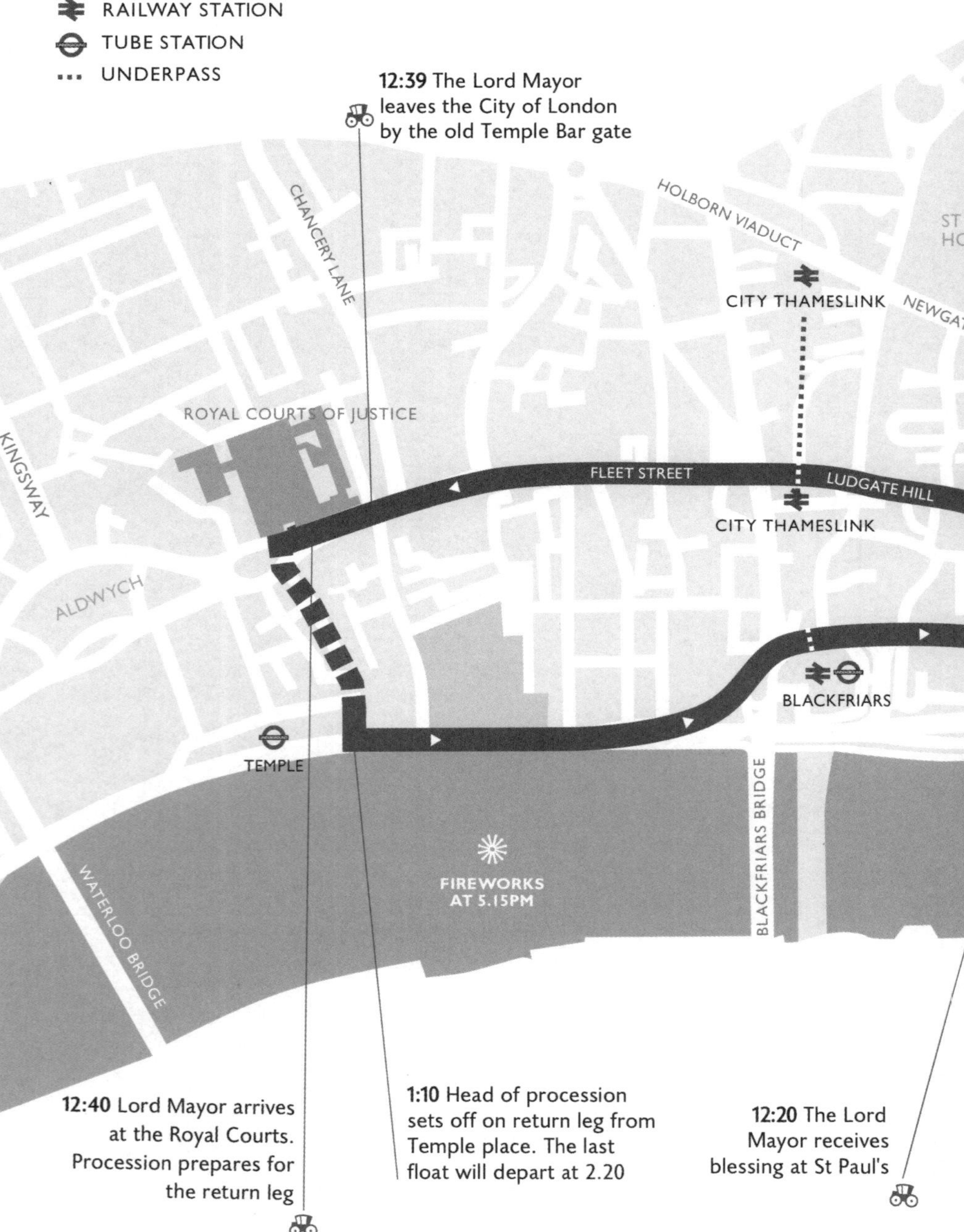

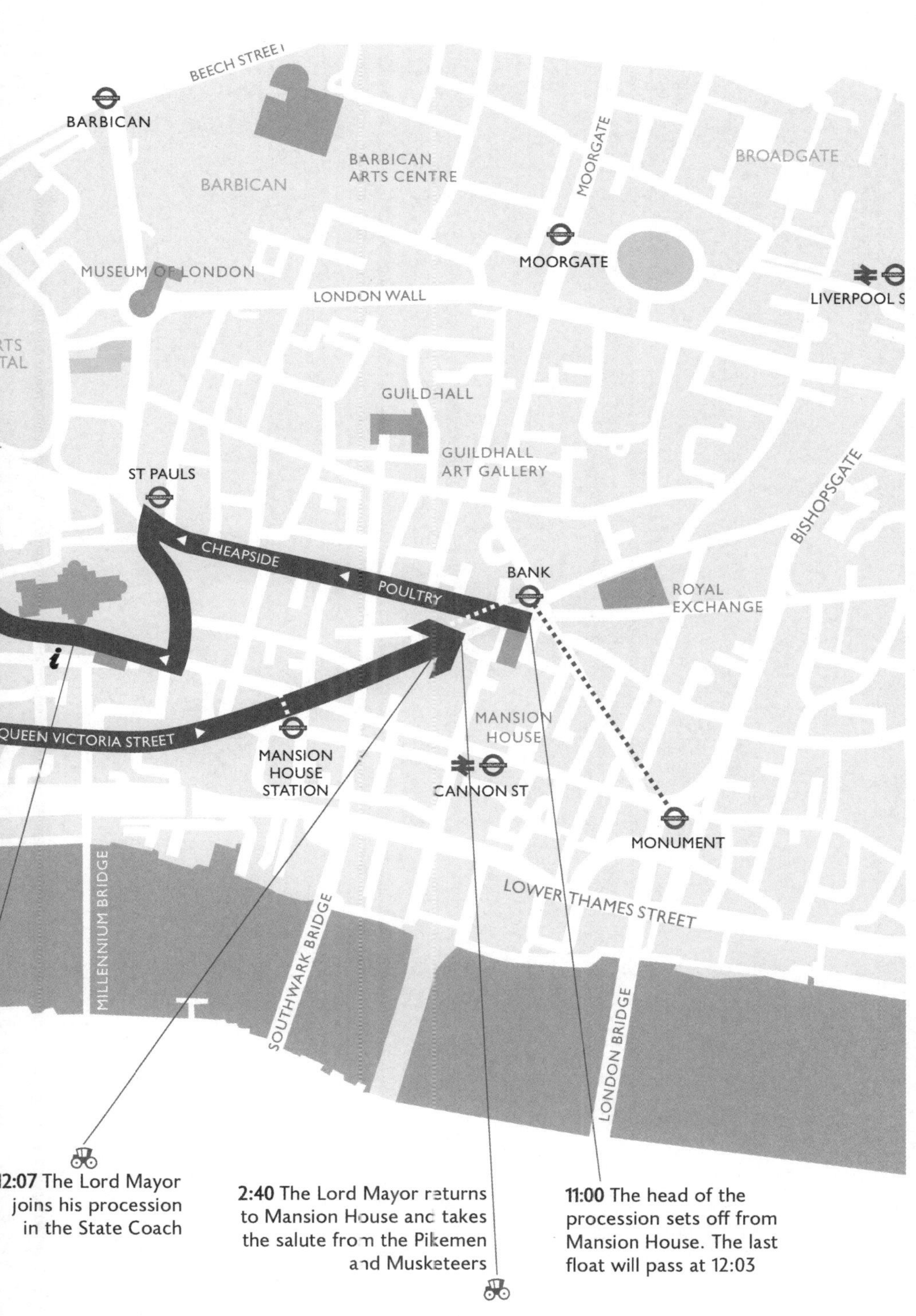

BEECH STREET
BARBICAN
BARBICAN
BARBICAN ARTS CENTRE
MOORGATE
BROADGATE
MUSEUM OF LONDON
MOORGATE
LONDON WALL
LIVERPOOL S
ARTS PITAL
GUILDHALL
GUILDHALL ART GALLERY
BISHOPSGATE
ST PAULS
CHEAPSIDE
POULTRY
BANK
ROYAL EXCHANGE
MANSION HOUSE
QUEEN VICTORIA STREET
MANSION HOUSE STATION
CANNON ST
MONUMENT
MILLENNIUM BRIDGE
SOUTHWARK BRIDGE
LOWER THAMES STREET
LONDON BRIDGE
12:07 The Lord Mayor joins his procession in the State Coach
2:40 The Lord Mayor returns to Mansion House and takes the salute from the Pikemen and Musketeers
11:00 The head of the procession sets off from Mansion House. The last float will pass at 12:03

Introduction

The first order, bellowed across the parade ground by the duty serjeant, is: 'Company of Pikemen and Musketeers – frame a body!'

More shouting from the duty serjeant and a long, ominous drumroll – everyone runs to their positions.

The drum stops with a final thump!

The P&Ms are standing at ease; the duty serjeant eyes them up and down.

'Have a care!'

They snap to attention. The duty serjeant addresses the ranks: 'Stand right in your files! Stand right in your ranks! Silence!'

The Company of Pikemen and Musketeers, aka the 'Company' or the 'P&Ms', is a ceremonial unit of the Honourable Artillery Company (the 'HAC') recruited from veterans of the HAC Army Reserve Regiment (the 'Regiment') wearing the uniforms of the HAC at the time of the English Civil War.

The HAC traces its origins to a charter granted by Henry VIII in 1537 to the Military Fraternity of St George, raising City volunteers to defend England from an invasion by France. At this point, HAC members were identified, from the ground in which they exercised, as 'Gentlemen of the Artillery Garden'. Their successors mobilised at Tilbury in 1588 to meet the Spanish Armada and in 1610 were confirmed by James I as an officer-producing unit for the City Trained Bands.

Over the next three centuries, the HAC evolved into a regiment in its own right, fighting in the Boer War and both world wars, providing Cold War reserves for the British Army of the Rhine and, since 1996, volunteers for active service.

This book provides a short tour through the history of the P&Ms, and with it the City of London, the HAC, and the nation itself.

Chapter One

1890–1924
The Halberdiers

In March 1890, the HAC held its thirty-third annual assault-at-arms at its HQ at Armoury House. There was boxing, swordplay, bayonet fighting and a recreation of the legendary quarterstaff duel between Robin Hood and Friar Tuck. Then came a special feature – a display of eighteenth-century halberd drill by six serving HAC infantrymen, dressed in authentic eighteenth-century uniforms and 'performing the drills laid down in Blackwell's 1726 compendium of military discipline as it is practised in the HAC'.

The HAC's new Halberdier Company was an immediate success and quickly booked to appear at other events, most importantly the Chelsea Royal Military Exhibition. This five-month long event, showcasing for the first time the history and traditions of the British Army, was opened on 4 July 1890 by Edward, Prince of Wales (later Edward VII) and visited in due course by Queen Victoria herself. The exhibition featured an outdoor display presented each day by a different military unit. The HAC's turn came on 23 July and the Halberdier Company again drew special attention. On 9 August 1890, the *Penny Illustrated Paper* reported:

> Far and away the most picturesque performance was the Halberdier exercise in the quaint and brilliant uniform of the Marlborough period, under the masterly direction of Captain

> Richard Birkett, whose stentorian voice was heard all over the gardens. This really splendid revival of old-time glories drew special enthusiasm of a veteran Sergeant Major who exclaimed with gusto, 'Ah! The Queen ought to witness this fine Halberdierian exercise at Osborne!'

Serving members of a military unit recreating their own history was a completely new concept in 1890 and drew extensive interest. The idea was picked up by the Royal Tournament in 1895 when it gave its first historical pageant – the Buffs (East Kent Regiment) appearing in the uniforms of their seventeenth-century musket and pike predecessors. The Lord Mayor's Show followed in 1896 with – 'England and Her Heroes' – a series of floats displaying men in army and naval uniforms from different periods of British history.

The HAC Halberdier Company continued to mount ceremonial displays and guards throughout the 1890s, including in 1895 a guard of honour for the Prince of Wales as guest of honour at an HAC smoking concert.[1] One of the original 1890 Halberdiers was Frank Farrington, a City clerk who had joined the HAC Infantry in 1883 and risen slowly through the ranks, becoming commanding officer of the HAC Infantry Battalion in 1907 and retiring finally in 1910.

Throughout Farrington's career, the HAC Infantry Battalion had worn the full dress Guards uniform of scarlet tunics and bearskins.

Then came the First World War and the British Army went to war in khaki. Farrington, aged 52, was too old for the front line but managed to obtain a post as training major with the HAC

---

1. A Victorian light entertainment for a usually male audience who chatted and smoked throughout.

recruiting battalion and later as commander of the Imperial Yeomanry Cadets.

By 1918, 13,000 HAC members had served on the Western Front, in the Middle East and in Italy, with 1,600 losing their lives. The same year, the HAC was revived as a Territorial Army (TA) unit, clad solely in khaki. Pre-war full dress uniforms were now seen as old-fashioned and anachronistic, though the Royal Tournament still included a regular pageant feature where regiments re-enacted their history, where the Grenadiers and Coldstreams portrayed their roles in the Restoration of King Charles II, and the Royal Marines their musket and pike drills of 1671.

So, thought Farrington, it should be possible for the HAC to have a ceremonial unit, manned by HAC members and reflecting the HAC's history and traditions, so long as it was presented as a piece of pageantry and not as the HAC Regiment on parade.

Farrington then used his considerable influence within the HAC to propose a revival of the old Halberdier Company. His proposal was supported by George Goold Walker ('GW'), the HAC secretary – with one major qualification. GW had discovered that the Halberdier Company was based on a misunderstanding of Blackwell's 1726 drill book. Halberds had only ever been carried by NCOs as a badge of office, and there had never been a Halberdier Company as such. Instead, he suggested that the reference date for the new company should be moved back to 1641, the year when the HAC first occupied the New Artillery Garden on Moorgate, and the period for which the earliest available HAC drill manuals were available.

Farrington found GW's logic unarguable. The HAC's Court of Assistants approved the revised proposal and a call went out for volunteers 'to perpetuate the pageantry of the past and revive in tangible form the earlier traditions of the HAC'.

Chapter Two

1610–1707
The First Pikemen and Musketeers

In the seventeenth century, England had no standing army and the HAC's citizen volunteers were the nearest it had to a military establishment. HAC members provided officers for the City Trained Bands and practised the postures of the pike and musket, first in the old Artillery Ground on Bishopsgate, and then the New Artillery Ground at Moorgate. The poet Ben Jonson, who had himself seen active service in the Low Countries, approved:

> Well, I say thrive, thrive brave Artillery Yard,
> Thou seed-plot of the war, that hast not spared
> Powder, or paper, to bring up the youth
> Of London, in the military truth,
> These ten years' day; as all may swear that look
> But on thy practice, and the posture book.[2]

The HAC was also a school of military theory, and several members wrote military textbooks. The most famous was William Barriffe's *Military Discipline*,[3] first published in 1635. Its frontispiece shows the

---

2. 'A Speech According to Horace', by Ben Jonson *ca.* 1626/7.

3. William Barriffe, *Military discipline: or, the yong artillery man Wherein is discoursed and showne the Postures both of Musket and Pike: the exactest way, &c. Together with the Motions which are to be used, in the excercising of a Foot-company. With divers and severall formes and figures of Battell; with their reducements.*

HAC coat of arms with, for the first time, a pikeman and musketeer as supporters. Goold Walker planned to bring the pikeman and the musketeer back to life.

When the Civil War began in 1642, the City had sided with Parliament. The HAC's keenest members volunteered for Parliament field regiments, among them William Barriffe, who became the major of Hampden's Greencoats, responsible for drill and deployment. Barriffe served at the Battle of Brentford and the siege of Reading and, when Hampden was killed in the spring of 1643, took over command, only to die in the typhus epidemic that swept through the Parliament army that summer.

Most HAC members served in the Lord Mayor's 'private army' – the six City Trained Bands, which could only be mobilised with the Lord Mayor's consent and which, at Parliament's request, fielded brigades at Turnham Green, Newbury and Cheriton. The performance of the HAC-officered City Brigade at Newbury in the face of royalist artillery fire and cavalry attack won the HAC its greatest accolade. Royalist historian Clarendon wrote:

> The London Trained Bands … (of whose inexperience of danger, or any kind of Service beyond the easy practice of their Postures in the Artillery Garden, Men had 'till then too cheap an estimation) behaved themselves to wonder; and were, in truth, the preservation of that Army that day. For they stood as a Bulwark and rampire to defend the rest.

The modern P&Ms wear their red coats as a tribute to the Red Trained Band at Newbury.

Perhaps a third of Civil War HAC members may have had royalist sympathies but in London, such views were dangerous. Only a few were brave enough to leave their homes to fight for the King, but there were enough of them to officer a royalist cavalry regiment and garrisons at Basing House and Faringdon.

After the Restoration, the HAC continued to officer the Trained Bands, which in turn provided a natural recruiting base for Charles II's first regular regiments, including:

- the Duke of York's Maritime Regiment, now the Royal Marines
- the 3rd Battalion Grenadier Guards, drawn from units originally raised, like the Royal Marines, by special warrant within the City
- Holland's Regiment of Foot, later the Royal East Kent Regiment (the Buffs), later part of the Queen's Regiment and now the Princess of Wales's Royal Regiment
- the 7th Battalion Royal Fusiliers, the lineal descendants of the Trained Bands.

The HAC's pikemen and musketeers provided the Lord Mayor with his personal bodyguard from at least the early seventeenth century. The poet Thomas Middleton described them on Lord Mayor's Day 1619:

The noble pains and loves of the heroic captains of the City and gentlemen of the Artillery Garden, making with two glorious Ranks a manly and Majestic passage for their Lord General, his Lordship, through Guildhall yard; and afterward their loves to his Lordship resounding in a second noble volley.[4]

---

4. Thomas Middleton, *The Triumphs of Love and Antiquity* (1619).

From 1657 onwards, the bodyguard role became a permanent one, still made up of pikemen and musketeers; though the bayonet was now beginning to render the pike obsolete. Status-conscious citizens preferred the pike as the more gentlemanly weapon and carried it into the early eighteenth century. Edward Ward's poem 'Battle without Bloodshed'[5] describes a City muster in 1701:

> Dub, dub, dubba dub, says the drum in the morning
> to give the bold heroes of London Town warning …
> To the 'Change or Guildhall a full gallop they run
> The tall man with pike and the short man with gun.

Ward did not have a high opinion of the pikemen:

> These poking old knaves armed with hop-poles and rapiers
> Are grocers and mercers, attorneys and drapers.
> Rich Cits of repute who a musket distaining
> As a load for a porter, yet crawl out a'training
> With what their old shoulders are able to carry
> And all for the City's great honour and glory.

In 1707, the HAC musketeers were finally issued with bayonets and pikemen disappeared for the next 218 years.

---

5. Edward Ward, 'Battle without Bloodshed; Or, Martial Discipline Buffoon'd by the City Train-Bands' (1701) printed in *The Second Volume of the Writings of the Author of the London Spy.*

Chapter Three

1925–1929
Early Days

By 1925, Farrington and Goold Walker had recruited and equipped twenty-four newly minted Pikemen. Nineteen were First World War veterans, mustering six MCs and two DSOs between them. Of the remaining five, three (including Farrington) had been too old for war service and two had been too young. Nine of the veterans, plus the two youngsters, were still serving in the HAC Regiment. Many were also in the HAC Division of the Metropolitan Special Constabulary (the 'Specials'), a part-time, unpaid volunteer police force formed in 1919 and headquartered at City Road Police Station.

GW was the adjutant and did all the organisation. Appointed secretary of the HAC in July 1922 and still in his early thirties, he was a thin, nervous man with enormous energy and organisational skills and, in the manner of the time, modest to the point of self-effacement. He had landed in France with the Royal Artillery (RA) in September 1915 and served at Loos, the Somme, Messines (where he won an MC), Arras, Vimy Ridge, Lens, Passchendaele (where he won a DSO) and in the pursuit to Mons.

The drumbeater was Percy Ayers, a wiry little man who had won an MC at Passchendaele when, as an RA forward observation officer (FOO), he had got ahead of the main attack and continued for many hours to send back fire directions from no man's land. After the war he had re-joined the HAC Regiment (he said) to play rugby, and joined the Pikes because it sounded like fun.

Frank Farrington was 'the Captain', a majestic figure in thigh-length boots, half armour and lobster pot helmet, with a flowing white moustache and magnificent head of white hair. Ayers recalled that 'he really looked most resplendent in his uniform and seemed to be made for the office, although his knowledge of our drill was scant.'

1925 duties

The Pikes did their first two duties in April 1925, providing guards of honour at the HAC Mess Club Civic Dinner (principal guest the Lord Mayor) and the HAC St George's Day dinner (tickets a costly 20*s.*).

Also in April, GW held a press call where he put the Pikemen through their paces, described them as a continuation of the Halberdiers and expressed the hope that they would soon be joined by a company of musketeers. Not since the original Halberdier Company had a regiment set up a ceremonial unit that provided a direct link with its early history, and the event drew considerable attention. Journalists described the Pikemen's armour and helmet plumes shining in the sun, while Drumbeater Ayers, a diminutive figure under his outsize slouch hat, long drum and big white gauntlets, was also much remarked on.

In May, the Company took part in the opening ceremony of the British Empire Exhibition at Wembley. In June it held its first ladies' evening (tickets 10/6), an event which later evolved into the Company's annual 'Feast'. In July, it provided a display of the 'postures of the pike' at the HAC Military Tournament and Sports Day, filmed by Pathé News and shown in cinemas across the country.

In November, GW achieved a coup when the new Lord Mayor, Sir William Pryke (uncle of Ensign of Pikemen Stanley Pryke), allowed the Company to resume the HAC's historic role as his personal bodyguard. On 9 November, the Pikes paraded at Blackfriars in brilliant sunshine to greet the Lord Mayor on his return from the Law Courts, and escort the coach back to Guildhall. Again, the event was shown on Pathé News.

In January 1926, members of the Company organised a Pikeman's children's party for local schoolchildren in Clerkenwell and Finsbury. The Lord Mayor attended with his Pike bodyguard and there was tea, a piano entertainment, balloons, caps, streamers, squeakers and musical chairs. The children's party soon became a regular HAC event, which, by 1930, was being attended by over 700 children and 250 adults.

In 1926, concern was expressed at the Pikemen's standard of drill and turnout:

> Each pikeman battle to control
> His undeveloped scaffold-pole
> And yet preserve upon his face
> A gaze serene and full of grace
> Their feathers nod upon the breeze
> Their garters fay about their knees
> At every step one hears the clanks
> And clash of metal from the ranks
> In fact their progress o'er the sward
> Is reminiscent of a Ford.

Monthly drill evenings were instituted and standards improved.

The Pikes' appearance at the 1925 Lord Mayor's Show had been so popular that they were asked back for 1926 and prominently featured in the show's advertisements. But this time, as Ayers recalled:

The heavens opened and we were drenched. The coach stopped just in time to allow the Lord Mayor slightly to open the window and give us a wave – closing the window as soon as possible. We then marched back to headquarters in pouring rain. Landing up at Armoury House with the officers and Pikemen looking like a lot of Red Indians from the dye which had come from their feathers.

The Company had discovered for the first (but not the last) time that armour rusts instantly on contact with raindrops, damp plumes leave red stains on steel morions and, when soft felt shoes become waterlogged, they lose their shape and start to fall apart. Such was the perceived problem that the Pikes declined to take part in the 1927 show. The City decided that it still wished to retain a Pike presence and, the day before Lord Mayor's Day 1927, asked the Company to appear next evening at the Lord Mayor's Banquet. A few hours later, the Pikes held an emergency meeting, at which Farrington was not present, and approved the request.

Farrington had not been able to attend the emergency meeting and, it seems, did not approve of this new involvement in civic ceremony. At the next committee meeting, he raged at not having been consulted and threatened to report this 'breach of protocol' to the HAC court. An equally furious Company secretary responded by offering to resign. Later at another meeting, a motion was passed resolving that the Company should seek to do more civic duties, not less. Eventually, Farrington backed down and the Pikes became a fixture at the Lord Mayor's Banquet for the rest of the interwar period. At the 1928 banquet, they encountered, for the first time, Winston Churchill, who was at that time Chancellor of the Exchequer in Stanley Baldwin's government.

Another 1930s' duty was the annual City dinner of the Royal Society of St George, later extended to include the national meetings of the Society at the Savoy: both regular bookings that continued until the late 1960s.

Other, one-off duties included guards of honour for a Royal Welch Fusiliers old comrades' dinner commemorating the Battle of Papadopoli, a visit by Edward, Prince of Wales to the HAC, and a guard of honour for the Mayor of Westminster at a civic reception at the Park Lane Hotel.

Chapter Four

1930s
An Age of Pageants

In the 1890s, the Halberdier Company had pioneered the idea of a body re-enacting its own history. In 1905, a pageant at Sherborne extended this into a new fashion of villages, towns and whole communities re-enacting their own history. Large casts of local people blurred the boundary between actor and spectator and brought the community's past to life in a magical dilation of historic time. It was also at Sherborne that the director of the pageant was first referred to as 'the Pageantmaster'.

'Pageantitis' reached the HAC twenty-five years later when Goold Walker was commissioned to produce a regimental pageant, performed by HAC members and portraying different periods of their history. The display began with a detachment of Tudor hand gunners, passed through the Civil War and ended with a scene from the Western Front – a platoon returning, dog-tired, from a spell in the front-line trenches, played by men (including Percy Ayers) who, just twelve years earlier, had still been serving in Flanders. This final scene had a particular impact on the audience. The war to end all wars was over, a great challenge had been faced and overcome, and peace was now restored.

In the Civil War section the Pikemen were joined for the first time by eight Musketeers, wearing morions and armed with swords and matchlocks, who performed the postures of the musket to the shouted commands of the Elder Serjeant: tamping powder and shot into the musket barrel with a ramrod; fixing the lighted match in the lock; presenting the musket upon its rest; at the order 'Give fire breast high!', pulling the trigger to flip the smouldering match into the flash pan; and – Bang! A musket volley!

It was noted that, with the addition of Musketeers, the Company now faithfully embodied the Musketeer and Pikeman on the HAC coat of arms.

GW's pageant was filmed by Pathé News and shown in cinemas across the nation. He received many further invitations to act as Pageantmaster and subsequently presented pageants at the 1932 Woolwich Garrison Searchlight Tattoo, the 1936 Lord Mayor's Show and the 1937 HAC 400th anniversary garden party. He also masterminded a special display at the 1937 Royal Tournament depicting an HAC field day of 1829, complete with scarlet coatees and bell-top shakos.

In 1933, the Pikes escorted the Lord Mayor on his visit to the Greenwich Night Pageant, a celebration of Greenwich as the birthplace of the Royal Navy, presented at the Royal Naval College by 2,500 performers and seen by 120,000 people (tickets 1s 6d to 12s 6d, with a fish dinner in the Painted Hall 5s 6d extra). The Pikemen met the Lord Mayor's state barge as he landed at the river steps and escorted him to the reception in the Painted Hall and afterwards at the main performance. This began with a group of elderly naval pensioners hobbling in, jesting and gossiping and then falling asleep – their dreams bringing to life the history of the Royal Navy, beginning with the christening of Queen Elizabeth I at Greenwich and ending with the death of Nelson.

In January 1935, the P&Ms took part in their first BBC outside radio broadcast: *An Evening at Armoury House*. The programme included a P&M drill display conveyed entirely by sound – the shouted order 'Have a care!' followed by the thud of feet hitting the floor as the Company came to attention. The broadcast was transmitted 'to our empire over the seas by means of waves in the air' and HAC expatriates from far away Malay and Rangoon wrote in to say how much they had enjoyed listening to those voices from home.

In 1935, GW took on his biggest commission ever – the history of the Tower of London (tickets 2*s*. to 21*s*.). Sponsored by the Tower Hill Improvement Fund, it took place over a fortnight in spring 1935, the audience sitting in stands overlooking the west moat, where a full stage set including a complete mediaeval street had been constructed.

The story began with Chaucer's pilgrims setting out from London for Canterbury. Among the players was Horace Pothecary, a small, impish man with a boylike face, known as Poth' or Pot. He had been called up in 1916 at the late age of 36 and fought in the HAC 2nd Battalion on the Western and Italian fronts. This was his first involvement with the HAC since 1918.

The pageant passed on through the centuries. Armoured knights levelled their lances and charged at each other, delighting the audience whenever one of them crashed to the ground with a great clang of armour. In 1415, Henry V's return after Agincourt was heralded by angelic choir boys singing the 'Agincourt Carol'. Afterwards they rampaged through the performers' tents like little demons, snatching (and wearing) the dainty shoes of the Elizabethan May Day revellers. In 1671, Captain Blood's attempt to steal the Crown Jewels went awry and he was knocked unconscious – his understudy had to take over for the rest of the run.

The P&Ms appeared in 1643 in a muster of the City Trained Bands, again in 1645 escorting Archbishop Laud to his execution on Tower Hill, and again in 1666 on crowd control duties at the Great Fire of London. But their *pièce de résistance* was a rendering of *Mars, his Triumph* – a drill display written by William Barriffe and first performed in 1638 at Merchant Taylors' Hall. The P&Ms began by framing a body and going through a series of formation drills. They were then attacked by a Saracen army who charged to the wild music of Mozart's *Il Seraglio* (Pothecary appearing again, now armed with a scimitar). Barbary guns and English muskets crashed out, followed by a free-for-all. One Saracen, hit on the nose by a musket butt, lost his temper and chased the offending Musketeer round the arena. Finally, a P&M ambush party took the Saracens in the flank and, after some more desperate scrapping, the P&Ms were victorious.

The Tower Pageant brought the P&Ms a surge of new recruits, among them Horace Pothecary, who signed up as a Musketeer, and the Company's establishment was increased, first from forty to fifty, and then to sixty.

In July 1936, forty-five P&Ms travelled to Huntingdonshire for the Hinchingbrooke Tattoo (referred to by the P&M as the Huntingdon Pageant), the Company's first duty outside London (tickets: seats 2*s.* 6*d.*; standing 1*s.*). Early in the morning they loaded mountains of kit into two charabancs and drove to Huntingdon, changed at the local Territorial Army centre and marched through the town with colours flying. The helmets worn by the Musketeers of 1930 had proved impractical for musket drill, and were now replaced with jaunty cavalier hats and wigs, with a strong flavour of Alexander Dumas.

Behind the main party came two 'sutlers' pushing a large wheelbarrow with a 6-gallon cask of beer – an image borrowed from 'Battle without Bloodshed':

> Then up comes a sutler whose trade is to cry
> A can of mild beer, who's a'dry who's a'dry?
> Here's stale beer and mild beer good stitch-back and pharaoh
> Though all his whole cellar is but a wheelbarrow.

On arrival at the Hinchingbrooke estate of the Earl of Sandwich, the Pikemen were mustered immediately for a drill display before they could get at the beer. A disappointed Pikeman muttered that, while 'we were doing our stuff the Musketeers were in assiduous attendance on that precious cask, to our unspeakable anguish'. His humour improved when it was the Musketeers' turn to perform, and the Pikes took possession of the barrel, quaffing ale from pewter tankards and puffing at seventeenth-century-style churchwarden pipes. 'We do not know who supplied the beer,' he opined, 'but it was rare, good stuff and saved our lives.'

In November 1935, the P&Ms provided a guard for a charity ball at the Savoy, in aid of the London Association for the Blind (tickets 2 guineas, including champagne). The event was held on Guy Fawkes Night and advertised as 'the Gunpowder Ball'. After supper, Guy Fawkes (played by one of the younger members of the Company) was spotted slinking round the edges of the room leaving gunpowder trails. The Pikemen gave chase, clanking along in their armour. Mr Fawkes gave them a good run for their money, setting fire to the gunpowder train just as they caught up with him and then putting up such a struggle that, before they could get clear, the gunpowder exploded 'with considerable éclat into the red plush seats of the Pikemen'.

Chapter Five

1932–1939
The Gathering Storm

In 1932, Hitler came to power, bringing with him the threat of war. The years since the Great War had seen dramatic developments in aerial warfare and Britain was uncertain how it would fare against a modern air attack. Prime Minister Stanley Baldwin warned that 'The bomber will always get through', and military historian Basil Liddell Hart predicted 250,000 casualties in the first week of an air war.

In 1936, the Lord Mayor's Show took as its theme 'The Defence of the Realm'. In contrast to GW's 1930 pageant, the challenge was no longer behind but ahead. World peace was under direct threat and the show portrayed London's past, present and future as a single continuum, the defenders of the past rallying with the defenders of the present to face the dangers of the future. This took the form of a Goold Walker-organised procession of soldiers (including the P&Ms) from different periods of London's history, followed at the end by modern TA regiments displaying their ability to defend London from air attack – Ack-Ack guns, searchlight lorries, cable layers, and a detachment from No. 600 City of London (Fighter) Squadron Auxiliary Air Force.

The next day the P&Ms appeared in one of the BBC's very first television broadcasts. Arriving at the Alexandra Palace, they encountered 'a seemingly hopeless tangle of cameras, lights, microphones, cables, ladders and a couple of dozen gentlemen in white coats whose job it was to put us on the air'. The transmission picked up on the 'Defence of the Realm' theme, the camera tracking up and down their ranks while the narrator described their uniforms, weapons and history. At the end, the spirits of England's defenders were shown marching through her history – an effect achieved by marching in circles round a camera, cunningly tilted to give a 'down the ages' effect.

In 1938, the Royal Tournament abandoned its traditional historical pageant in favour of a display of modern battlefield skills. P&Ms in the Specials were being trained to deal with air raids and poison gas attack. The Air Raid Precautions ('ARP') Act had come into force in January and ARP wardens were being recruited, air raid shelters built and gas masks issued. Pikeman Major R.A. (Richard) Robinson (a local government official who had served with the HAC 2nd Battalion alongside Pothecary in France and Italy) became chief ARP officer in charge of air defence for Middlesex.

In December 1938, the P&Ms appeared at Salters' Hall for the installation of the Master of the Gold and Silver Wyre Drawers. Four Musketeers and six Pikemen were posted on the grand stair. Lord Kennet, proposing the Master's health, said that he didn't think the P&Ms' weapons were much of a contribution to rearmament. A P&M responded by claiming that a half pike, properly deployed, could see off an entire air raid.

The theme of England's past and present, coming together to defend her future, reappeared in the Finchley Tattoo of July 1938 and the Wimbledon Searchlight Tattoo of June 1939, where the P&Ms took part in a procession of citizen volunteers portraying every period of England's history. 'Nearly a thousand years have passed', said the echoing voice on the Tannoy, 'since English folk last saw the campfires of a hostile army in their island, but many have tried, and in every crisis, it is to her citizens that England looks for aid.'

The challenge of the future was forcefully represented by the acting out of an actual air raid, described by the voice on the Tannoy:

> The peace of a market day in Wimbledon is shattered by the whine of an air raid siren – ARP wardens rush to guide people to their shelters and a TA convoy drives into the arena and deploys its Ack-Ack guns and searchlights. An enemy plane appears overhead; the searchlights pick it up and the guns begin to fire.

The narrator goes on to describe a first aerial attack with high explosive, a second with incendiaries, and a third with poison gas. As the raid finishes, decontamination squads and first-aid parties rush out to deal with the casualties.

Two months later, on 3 September 1939, Britain finally declared war. Every national resource was now directed to the war effort and many P&Ms made personal contributions.

Frank Farrington re-joined the HAC Court of Assistants as chairman of the Estates Committee, busy preparing Armoury House for air attack – boarding up windows, hanging blackout curtains, piling sandbags around doorways, sending the regimental treasures to safe storage in the country, installing a searchlight in the Artillery Ground and tethering a barrage balloon above it.

GW re-joined the Royal Artillery and was posted to Uxbridge, the HQ of Air Vice Marshal Keith Park's No. 11 Group, the main RAF formation defending the south-east of England. Here, his role was to act as senior liaison officer between 11 Group and the Anti-Aircraft (AA) units guarding London and the south coast.

Another fourteen P&Ms were serving in the Specials, headed by Pikeman Assistant Commander F.Y. (Frank) Bright. He had served on the Western Front with the Royal Artillery and been wounded at Loos. Of vast physical dimensions, ponderous and rocklike, with a strong sense of personal dignity, he had never reconciled with his nickname of 'Fanny', derived from his F.Y. initials. His constables included Police Sergeant Ayers and Special Constable Pothecary. On the declaration of war, they were all posted to Commercial Street Police Station on the edge of the Docks, where they were soon busy enforcing the blackout, evacuating children to the country (Operation Pied Piper), registering aliens and issuing ration books.

A dozen more P&Ms mobilised in the HAC's National Defence Companies (NDCs), a home service version of the TA. Their commander was Pikeman John Bamford Smith (known as 'JB') who had served with the HAC guns in Palestine and had been one of the original 1925 Pikemen. Later, the HAC NDCs merged with the Royal Berkshire (Hackney) NDCs to form 13th (Home Service) Royal Fusiliers, a battalion-strong formation with JB as its new commanding officer. At its peak, it mustered 1,500 men and 120 officers, guarding vulnerable points across London and also providing the resident garrison (under Pikeman Tony Antunovitch) at the Bank of England.

Months passed and nothing happened. Towards the end of 1939, Antunovitch asked the HAC Court of Assistants if they could lend his garrison a billiard table to help pass the time. After some spluttering, the Court agreed.

Over in Commercial Street, the members of the Specials were rostering two or three times a week, coming on duty in the evening, walking the beat until the early hours of the morning, catching a few hours' sleep under a blanket on the station floor and then back to the day job.

For Horace Pothecary, a lifelong bachelor and teetotaller, life in a wartime police station was infinitely preferable to his bachelor rooms in Wimbledon. Rationing had begun in January 1940 but in the Commercial Street police canteen you could still get a good supper of (unrationed) corned beef and hot mashed potatoes, washed down with milky tea and as much (unrationed) sugar as you liked. Then a slow, 12-mile foot patrol around Stepney, back to Commercial Street and a short, untroubled sleep in a 'remarkable Heath Robinson "Poth-Nest" of his own invention, composed of clothes racks, blankets, wire and string'. In the morning, breakfast in the canteen (unrationed bacon and eggs, bread and butter and unrationed jam, more tea with more unrationed sugar), then a longish walk to his office in the West End for a day's work and back at the station in the evening. He never missed a single duty. An astonished Bright found himself breaking into verse:

> The legions had departed and the eagles all had flown,
> But Lictor Pothecarius was somehow left alone,
> so he painted up his helmet in a pleasing shade of woad
> And started in patrolling up along the Hackney road.

In May 1940, Hitler launched his Blitzkrieg and the 'phoney war' was over. The Germans swept across France and the British fled back across the Channel. Invasion was now imminent, with landings expected on the south coast, supported by parachutists and glider troops attacking inland.

To meet the airborne invasion threat, fourteen P&Ms now joined the newly formed Home Guard. Among them was Drumbeater Ayers, who left the Specials for his local Home Guard unit in Bromley, the 51st Kents, where he became captain and weapons officer. Bromley was part of the Outer London Defence Ring and the 51st Kents spent the first weeks of their existence building pillboxes and digging tank traps, while Ayers made Molotov cocktails to throw at the German tanks when they arrived.

JB's Fusiliers became the London Docks Garrison, defending the East End from sabotage, German parachute landings and river-borne attack. His rear HQ was at 22 Bunhill Row, a new bomb disposal section was installed at 23 Bunhill Row and a new forward HQ in a police station just outside the West India Docks gate. The rest of his eight companies were distributed around the West India, East India, Royal and Surrey Docks.

On 10 July, the Germans began Operation Eagle Attack to destroy Britain's air defences. At Park's Uxbridge HQ, 50 feet below ground, GW was in the glass-fronted gallery overlooking the main operations room, listening to messages coming in from the Observer Corps and radar stations, reporting when the Ack-Ack batteries on the Thames Estuary opened fire, and signalling them to hold fire as the RAF's fighters took to the air.

At Bromley, the 51st Kents were in position within seven minutes of the siren sounding. Ayers and the other HQ officers watched from the roof of Bromley Police Station as German bombers attacked Biggin Hill a few miles to the north, the attack spilling over to Bromley, where the 51st Kents claimed to have brought down a Dornier with rifle fire.

Chapter Six

1940–1945
The Battle of London

Luftwaffe attacks on RAF aerodromes continued throughout July and August, with No. 11 Group bearing the brunt of it. In September, Hitler switched to London, where perhaps half of the Pikemen and Musketeers were now serving in some form of uniformed air defence role.

On 7 September, around 5 pm, JB was driving back along the Highway to West India Docks when 300 German bombers appeared in the sky ahead. As the bombs began to fall he and his driver took cover. But when the raid showed no sign of stopping, he got back in the car, drove though the fire to his Docks HQ, and set about telephoning his companies and issuing orders.

At 8 pm, just as the Specials were coming on duty at Commercial Street, a second, much heavier raid began and the code word 'Cromwell' went out, signalling 'Invasion imminent'. JB put everyone on high alert and posted a strong force at the east end of King George V Dock to meet any attack coming up the Thames. At the Bank, Antunovitch manned the Lewis machine guns on the roof, looking for German parachutists. In Bromley, Ayers opened his weapons locker and started issuing Molotovs.

There was no invasion that night, but in the morning, 9 miles of waterfront were ablaze. The air was choked with the smell of burning warehouses and their contents – grain, timber, tea, rubber, oil, paint, tar, soap, varnish, all bound together with water from the firemen's hoses. Flames from the Woolwich munitions factory and Beckton Gas Works danced across the horizon.

In the afternoon, there was another incendiary raid, followed by another nighttime raid using the fires started by the incendiaries as target markers. JB was again at the centre of the attack, scores of bombs falling all around his dugout, noise deafening, walls shaking violently, oil lamps swinging and nearly going out. When the raid ended, there was a moment of eerie silence, soon broken by the tinkling of fire engine and ambulance bells.

On the second night, Rum Quay was hit and the 1,000-foot long warehouse complex was soon blazing from end to end. 'Amazing sight,' wrote JB. 'The flames seemed to rush along the whole great length of the warehouse, screaming almost more than roaring, intermingled with batches of small explosions.' One and a quarter million gallons of blazing rum flowed over the side of the quay and onto the surface of the water, setting light to the barges.

Another time, JB was on the river when the raid began.

> I watched as [the bombers] approached over the top of Tower Bridge … bursts of flame and clouds of smoke and dust on north and south sides – with great geysers of water blown up when one fell in the river … houses were being hit on all sides – a great warehouse on the south shore of the river got one full in its vitals and went down like a blazing pile of child's toy bricks.

Over in Commercial Street, as soon as the raid eased off, the Specials were out setting up perimeters, directing ambulance and fire services, digging out survivors, evacuating residents, organising relief centres and chasing off looters. The station landlines were humming – reports coming in of a suspected parachutist landing (it turned out to be parachute mines), burst gas and water mains, and full-scale disasters. A direct hit on the Peabody Estate, just down the road from the station, killed seventy-eight residents sheltering in the basement. Towards dawn, a bleary-eyed Assistant Commander Bright handed over to his regular police relief and lumbered off to his office in Great Portland Street for a few hours' sleep. On the way out he passed Poth' on the front desk answering a missing person enquiry. 'Nothing under that name on my lists, Madam; let's hope for the best.'

The Luftwaffe attack on the Docks continued for five days and nights. On the fourth day, JB recorded that everyone was still doing their jobs very willingly – the problem was lack of sleep. His elderly volunteers could not continue indefinitely without sleep.

Some relief came on 12 September when the Germans expanded their attack to the City. That afternoon, a huge, 1-ton delayed-action bomb landed in front of the west steps of St Paul's and dug itself into the soft London clay. JB's 23 Bunhill Row bomb squad spent the next three days digging it out. JB wrote in his war diary:

> Bomb weighed a ton, was down 27½ feet, had broken and fired a gas main in its descent. Lt Davis with his men dug the bomb out, loaded it onto a lorry, and Davis himself drove the lorry to Hackney Marshes, where he exploded it. There is no doubt that Davis by his successful work saved St Paul's Cathedral from very severe damage.

The church of St Augustine's & St Faith's, Watling Street, was less important and less lucky. On the night of 9 September, a shower of high explosive bombs damaged its tower and destroyed most of its nave. The church was empty apart from the rector's cat, Faith, who had recently moved herself and her kitten Panda into the relative safety of the cellar, where they were buried under the rubble. The next morning, the rector, searching the ruins, heard a mewing from beneath the debris and managed to dig them out, alive and unharmed but very dusty, just before the roof collapsed on the space where they had been sheltering.

Up in the air, the Battle of Britain was reaching a climax. On 15 September, a massive German attack was met head-on by GW's Ack-Ack gunners and No. 11 Groups' fighters; and the Luftwaffe suffered a major defeat. This day in September, now commemorated as Battle of Britain Day, was a turning point. There would be no invasion in 1940 … perhaps not ever.

Those who served in the London Blitz – JB's Fusiliers, the Specials and thousands of others, when they had a moment to draw breath, were astonished to find that the bombing, intended to create panic and disorder, had instead brought them closer together and made them more determined to win. On 23 September, King George VI addressed the nation over the wireless:

> It is not the walls that make the City, but the people who live within them. The walls of London may be battered, but the Spirit of the Londoner stands resolute and undismayed.

In November, the pressure eased again as the Luftwaffe expanded its attack to the rest of Britain. Around this time, as the Docks became less dangerous, JB began to receive VIP visits, first from the Duke of Kent (arriving at King George V Dock while bombs were still dropping) and then Churchill and the King. All were amazed that a scratch regiment of over-the-hill veterans had held together, cheerfully and without faltering, throughout the Luftwaffe onslaught.

Soon afterwards, the 13th Royal Fusiliers were removed to North London to recuperate.

In December 1940, Farrington placed a Christmas message in the *HAC Journal*:

> Colonel F. Farrington, on behalf of the members of the Company of Pikemen & Musketeers, sends greetings and best wishes to the members of the Company who are once again serving with the Forces, and trusts that the day is not far distant when they will once again muster to the sound of the drumbeater. 'Have a Care!'

The Battle of London resumed on Sunday, 29 December, when a heavy night raid raised a firestorm that destroyed a third of the City. St Paul's survived, but the Paternoster Row area north of the cathedral vanished in flames, Guildhall and its Art Gallery were set on fire, and nine Wren churches were damaged or destroyed. At Armoury House an incendiary went through the top of the west wing and set light to the Billiard Room, and houses along the west and south sides of the Ground were reduced to ruins. In the morning, Farrington's Estates Committee went immediately to work, organising repairs, filing war damage claims and negotiating ground rent reductions with bombed-out tenants.

A few days later, JB's garrison at the Bank of England phoned on the landline to report 'a helluva bomb bang in the middle of the bank crossing … looks as if it's blown the whole road to blazes'. The bomb had exploded in the booking hall of Bank tube station, the blast travelling though the subways and escalators, killing fifty-two people and leaving a vast crater in the middle of the Mansion House interchange. JB was shocked by the carnage, but heartened by the way everyone immediately set about repairing the damage: 'A kind of suspension bridge was thrown over almost at once … and in an amazingly short while – considering the enormous damage, the great crater was covered over and traffic running fairly normally.'

The Blitz continued through the winter and into the spring. Mansion House, the Old Bailey and the Tower of London were all hit, JB's business premises behind Fishmongers Hall were bombed to bits. Armoury House was hit several more times – windows were blown in, the drill hall roof was blown off twice, a blast brought down part of the front portico, and two of JB's Fusiliers were killed. Over at Commercial Street, the police station took a direct hit and Commandant Fanny Bright's office was destroyed, though amazingly there were no casualties.

By the spring, the Luftwaffe was moving east for the invasion of Russia and the raids finally died away. Between September 1940 and May 1941, London had endured 95 day raids and 166 night raids; 20,000 Londoners had been killed and 300,000 houses destroyed.

The London Blitz was Farrington's last tour of duty. In June 1941 he died in his sleep, aged 79. The same month, Goold Walker was posted to Suffolk to train a new Light Anti-Aircraft Battery. When his battery was posted overseas (Tunisia) he was left behind as too old. In 1942 he reached the military age limit of 50 and returned, rather mournfully, to his old job at Armoury House. Air raid damage and occupation by JB's bomb section had rendered his accommodation at 23 Bunhill Row uninhabitable, so the HAC paid him an allowance in lieu. But when the Inland Revenue decided to tax this as income, the HAC hurriedly converted the basements and ground floors of 23 and 24 Bunhill Row into a makeshift (non-taxable) apartment for him to live in.

By 12 August 1941, Special Constable Pothecary had completed 700 duties – every day since the start of the war except two Christmas Days when Fanny Bright (now Commandant Bright) had closed the doors and expressly forbade him to go near the place.

Elsewhere, the Home Guard was being upgraded and expanded to take over home defence and free up regular units for overseas service. In Bromley, Ayers was given command of a new mobile reserve, which could be rushed to any point where an enemy airborne landing had been detected. His transport was made up of civilian motor cars, motorcycles, a lorry and a bus. And GW returned to the fray as a newly minted lieutenant colonel, commanding a City of London AA group of four rocket batteries. As he said later: 'They decided I was too old for a major's job with pay so they gave me a lieutenant colonel's job (without pay) in the Home Guard with about a ten times larger command.'

In June 1942, JB was stood down as commanding officer of 13th Royal Fusiliers and posted to a desk job at RAF Cardington as army representative for the selection of army glider pilots for the invasion of Europe. In May 1943, he was fully retired, it being noted that he was 'well over the age limit for his rank'.

November 1943 saw the return of the Lord Mayor's Show in muted form. The new Lord Mayor, Sir Frank Newson-Smith, drove to the Law Courts in a closed car with his mace bearer and common cryer crammed inside, followed by a mayoral procession of six mobile anti-aircraft guns. Peals rang out as they passed St Lawrence Jewry in Gresham Street and St Mary-le-bow in Cheapside. The bells of both churches had been destroyed in the Blitz, but for the show, loudspeakers had been placed in the bell towers playing recordings of bell peals at top volume.

Wartime regulations had replaced the grandeur of the Lord Mayor's Guildhall Banquet with a much cheaper austerity luncheon at Mansion House. Seeking some additional, inexpensive element of display, Newson-Smith asked for a P&M guard of honour. The P&Ms hurriedly retrieved their uniforms and equipment from storage in Buckinghamshire where, to their dismay, they found their kit had been badly stored and everything was much damaged by damp and infestation. The uniforms were mouldy, the muskets rusted solid, and a mouse had nested in Drumbeater Ayers's hat. But with some frantic sponging, pressing and polishing, eighteen more or less presentable P&Ms paraded at Mansion House; the return of the 'scarlet-clad Pikemen' being particularly noted by the press.

The guest of honour was Prime Minister Winston Churchill who strode in, hands pressed in pockets and jaw out-thrust, along the corridor of Pikemen. Later, the P&Ms led the guests into the Egyptian Room before retiring to the balcony to listen to the speeches, where an upbeat Churchill spoke of Britain's recent series of almost unbroken victories in Africa, Sicily and Italy.

In 1944, the air threat returned in the shape of Hitler's new flying bombs. This, and the fear of German paratrooper attack, kept Ayers and the Home Guard in service through most of 1944, and persuaded the City to cancel the Lord Mayor's Show.

In November, with the Allies advancing across Europe, the Home Guard was finally disbanded. One of Ayers's last acts was the delivery of his arms and armaments to the nearest weapons dump, including all his Molotovs. At the HAC, 1940-vintage Molotovs were considered so unstable that they were simply buried in the north-east corner of the Ground. The final act came in 1945 when the Specials left Commercial Street to return to their peacetime station in City Road.

The Battle of London was, for those who fought in it, an intense, dangerous, front-line campaign. But it did not count as active service, and there was no campaign medal.[6] There were some 'non-operational gallantry awards'. Lieutenant Robert Davis RE (later cashiered for

---

6. There was eventually a generic Defence Medal for civil defence, home guard, police, fire services and non-operational military service in the UK under air attack 1939–45.

embezzling military funds) got a GC (George Cross) for digging out the big bomb from under the west front of St Paul's. JB got an OBE (Order of the British Empire) for his tenacious defence of the Docks. R.A. Robinson got another OBE for his leadership of the Middlesex ARP, and Poth' got a BEM (British Empire Medal) for never missing a duty throughout the entire war.

The fortitude of Faith the cat was deemed ineligible for the Dickin Medal (the animal equivalent of a Victoria Cross) because she was not a military cat. To address this lacuna, Maria Dickin, who had founded the People's Dispensary for Sick Animals back in 1917, created a new 'civilian' animal medal, which was awarded to Faith for her courage and steadfastness in the Battle of London. In October 1945, in the ruins of St Augustine's, Archbishop of Canterbury Geoffrey Fisher held Faith in his arms while Maria Dickin hung the medal around her neck.

Chapter Seven

1945–1949
Hard Times

Austerity

Britain was victorious but desperately poor. For six years, she had channelled all her wealth into the war effort, abandoned her export markets, and relied on loans from the US, which would take decades to repay. National spending was dominated by US interest payments and, when she should have been rebuilding her economy, she was pouring more money into European reconstruction and defence.

Post-war austerity extended to every aspect of public and private life. Food, petrol, construction, entertainment and public events were all heavily controlled. Meat, sugar, eggs, dairy products, bread and flour – all the staples apart from potatoes – were still rationed. Fresh fruit and vegetables, fish and game were unrationed but hard to come by. Restaurant meals were limited to three courses, only one of which could be meat.

Drumbeater Ayers (a little stouter with the passage of time and now known as 'Tubby'), recently elected chair of the HAC's sutling (catering) committee, put out an appeal to members to sell any food surpluses they had to the HAC – home-grown fruit and vegetables, home-reared chickens, fish and game. There was a good response and, in the bleak post-war world, a lunch at Armoury House became something to look forward to (though the drinks were considered expensive – 9*d*. for a pint of beer and 1*s*. for a pink gin).

From Australia, retired Musketeer H.W. Hollidge wrote that unlimited milk, butter, cream and eggs were available, with no ration coupons needed for meat, sugar or anything else. Half-starved Britons could place orders for Australian food parcels with Barry & Roberts, a major Australian department store. Cheaper food parcels could be ordered through the Lord Mayor's Mansion House scheme, but with no choice as to contents. The government did its bit by decreeing that parcels weighing more than 5lb would be deducted from the recipient's ration entitlement.

Just after the ferocious winter of 1946/47, the P&Ms held their first post-war Feast, the meal limited to the three courses prescribed by law but decent enough by the standards of the time. It began with tomato soup, almost certainly tinned given the harshness of the preceding winter, then a main course of roast chicken (a delicacy), creamed potatoes and cauliflower – all ably supported by Tubby's network of home producers. Finally, a particular treat – a portion of Neapolitan ice cream divided into strips of strawberry, chocolate and vanilla.

Half the City was still in ruins. Building materials and labour were centrally controlled and there were no licences for commercial rebuilding. City bombsites were cleared of rubble and dangerous areas boarded up, but that was about it. At Guildhall, the burnt-out shells of the Great Hall and the Art Gallery had been patched up and covered with temporary tin roofs. Salters' Hall, where the P&Ms had paraded in 1938, had been bombed flat in 1941 and was still a pile of ruins.

The government's priority was residential housing. The P&Ms joined in, in the 'Silver Lining Campaign' in 1947. Run by the National Savings Committee, it aimed to raise £366 million to finance residential accommodation. The P&Ms had paraded for the National Savings

Movement in its 1944 'Salute the Soldier' campaign when public spirit was at its height, and savings campaigns almost the only permitted form of public display. In those days, the movement had had huge public support but now, with the war over, support was less certain.

The National Savings Committee enlisted Field Marshal Montgomery, escorted by the Pikemen, to make the biggest impact possible at the opening ceremony at Guildhall. The Company advanced pikes, Montgomery made an uninspiring speech ('I accepted [the invitation to take part] because I always do what I am told by the government') and the campaign was under way. After six months, it had sold only £67 million of savings certificates against a projected target of £161 million. The National Savings Committee noted the half-hearted response and did not attempt a major campaign again.

Politics

Meanwhile, a new organisation was in the headlines. The United Nations (UN) had been formed by Franklin D. Roosevelt and Winston Churchill in 1945 to guarantee world peace, by providing a forum for international cooperation and agreement. The UN's first full general assembly, attended by fifty-one nations, met in January 1946 in London where an impoverished government struggled to provide a suitable welcome. The Home Secretary asked the City to help by giving a banquet, and the City asked the P&Ms along to make it look a bit grander.

The P&Ms had come back together quickly after the war and were now thirty-five strong, composed almost entirely of Pikemen (wartime storage had badly damaged many of the muskets). Twenty-five Pikemen duly paraded for the UN delegates inside the fire-blackened walls of Guildhall, where the new prime minister, Clement Attlee, spoke of the new world the UN would usher in, governed by justice and the moral law.

With world security and freedom now assured, Britain began to disarm, indifferent to events in Eastern Europe, where Stalin was busy converting his occupied territories into Soviet satellites. Then, in March 1946, at Fulton, Missouri, Churchill delivered his famous warning: 'From Stettin in the Baltic to Trieste in the Adriatic, an iron curtain has descended across the continent.' People listened to Churchill, and reluctantly began to re-arm against the Soviet threat.

An early step was the revival in January 1947 of the Territorial Army, and with it the HAC active service regiment. Field Marshal Lord Alanbrooke, the HAC's new Colonel Commandant, led a recruiting drive in which he warned of the continuing need for air defence, now that 'the power and intensity of aerial weapons has increased out of all proportion'. One of his first appointments was Edward Heath, an aspiring young politician who had served in the war with 86th (HAC) HAA Regiment Royal Artillery in Belgium, and now became CO of its successor regiment – 2nd AA Regiment HAC (HAA).

Europe was now divided into two power blocs, facing off against each other along the line of Churchill's Iron Curtain, testing and prodding for signs of weakness. The centre of the line ran through Germany – on one side East Germany and East Berlin controlled by Stalin, on the other, West Germany and West Berlin controlled by the West.

With American and British support, West Germany's economy revived rapidly, culminating in June 1948 with the introduction of its own currency, the Deutsche Mark. A furious Stalin responded by cutting off ground access to West Berlin and issuing an ultimatum: West Germany must either abandon the Deutsche Mark or hand West Berlin over to Russia. He thought the West had no appetite for a fight but, to his surprise, America and Britain responded with the

Berlin Airlift – a huge project that supplied West Berlin from the air for the next eleven months.

At home, the Soviet threat brought a surge of new volunteers and, for the first time, Heath's 2nd Regiment was recruited up to strength. Heath himself fully expected to be sent to defend West Germany. In August 1948, he wrote that everyone he knew was 'quite determined that if war comes, we shall have to show these tiresome people that they can't behave like this'.

This newly warlike mood, and the revival of the TA in particular, was reflected in P&M bookings. On 6 November 1948, they paraded in the Artillery Ground for the inauguration of the newly formed Royal Marines Forces Volunteer Reserve, their presence specially requested by the Royal Marines Commandant General to mark the HAC's historic connection with the original sea soldiers of the 1660s. A week later, they were marching in the Lord Mayor's Show, where the theme was 'The Auxiliary Forces of the Crown' – a visual acting out of the call for volunteers to join the TA.

In April 1949, the Pikes escorted the Lord Mayor at a full muster of the City's Auxiliary and Cadet Forces in the Artillery Ground, where the troops were so numerous that the Lord Mayor lost his way among the lines and inspected parts of the formation twice over. Also in April, the US, Britain and ten other nations sidestepped the UN and formed NATO, to defend Europe from Soviet imperialism.

In May 1949, Stalin gave in and lifted the blockade of West Berlin. But he was also busy developing his own atom bomb and, with the help of a network of spies and traitors, was able to conduct his first nuclear tests in August. This was bad news but, with the immediate threat of war over, everyone had relaxed. In October 1949, the Lord Mayor attended the P&Ms' annual feast (Ye Feast) for the first time as their guest of honour. At the Lord Mayor's Show in November, the theme was 'Transport through the Ages,' with Londoners getting out their old bangers and boneshakers for a jolly drive in the rain.

The Show

The first post-war Lord Mayor's Show had been held in November1945, when austerity was at its most severe. Everything was in short supply except military personnel, and the procession was a mass of khaki, navy blue and air force grey. The Lord Mayor's theme – 'The City's Privileged Regiments' – consisted of more soldiers in khaki. But in amongst the drabness came a splash of Venetian red marching twenty strong – the Pikemen were back for the first time since 1936.

In 1946 the theme was slightly livelier – 'Work and Play' (people walking or exercising in sports kit) – and, marvellous to behold, the Lord Mayor's gold coach, back from wartime storage in Newbury. How to make the most of it? Before the war it had been escorted by a troop of mounted cavalry, usually lancers or hussars, and latterly by the Household Cavalry. But in 1946, no cavalry of any kind was available, so the escort was provided by a detachment of Pikemen, their armour drawing humorous cries of 'Any old iron!' – the call of the rag-and-bone man.

In November 1947, the theme was 'Country Comes to Town' with floats displaying a plethora of home-grown produce, much of it, alas, heavily rationed or difficult for Londoners to come by. A float with John Bull standing on top of a vast pile of potatoes proved particularly controversial. Britain's potato crops had been devastated in the harsh winter of 1946/47 and from December onwards, potatoes, until now the only unrationed food staple, would be limited to 3lb (1.4kg) per person per week.

Nineteen forty-seven was also the year when the Lord Mayor's Show was formally recognised as a state event and the Pikes now marched, not only behind, but also alongside the mayoral coach. This 'coach party' formation was modelled on the Sovereign's Escort provided by the Yeomen of the Guard, most notably at the opening of Parliament, when a party of four Yeomen marched 'two and two', dressing off each of the coach wheels. The P&M coach party had four Pikemen dressing off the coach wheels, and two more in the middle alongside the Lord Mayor. Now, whenever anyone saw the Lord Mayor waving his hat out of the window, they would also see a line of Pikemen marching beside him – an instant image of City confidence and prosperity.

Public interest was apparent three days later when the P&Ms appeared live on the BBC television programme *Picture Page* in a feature on the Lord Mayor's Show. The tangle of cameras, lights, microphones, cables and ladders had barely changed since 1936, though the technicians no longer wore white laboratory coats.

At this time the Lord Mayor's Show still followed its original Victorian route, beginning at the saluting base at the entrance to Guildhall Yard, then proceeding down Gresham Street and into the City where it marched through the ward of the new Lord Mayor, returning via Mansion House Crossing to Queen Victoria Street, along the south side of St Paul's and down Ludgate Hill.

The brakes on the mayoral coach consisted of two officers in mufti walking behind and clinging on to the rear wheels if it went too fast – on its first post-war outing it sped up going down Ludgate Hill and nearly overran the horses. As this was also the first appearance of the Pikes behind the coach, a journalist from *The Scotsman* concluded that they were there to act as additional brakemen, provoking a suitably stuffy letter of correction from the P&M adjutant.

From Ludgate Hill, the procession entered Fleet Street, arriving at the Law Courts around midday. Around 1 pm, the procession re-formed and continued down the Strand towards Westminster Hall, where the Lord Mayor went to swear his oath before the Law Courts were built. They turned off Trafalgar Square down Northumberland Avenue, then onto the Embankment and marched back along Queen Victoria Street to Mansion House, where the Lord Mayor debussed. The Pikes went back to Armoury House and collapsed into armchairs in front of the Long Room fires for a couple of hours. In the early evening, they marched back down to Guildhall to provide the guard of honour at the Lord Mayor's Banquet, a gruelling duty of some eleven hours and 10 miles on foot and in armour.

Royal

In 1830, King William IV had instructed the HAC 'to consider themselves in future his bodyguard, by whom alone, it is expected, his Majesty will be attended in the City at the civic festival'. The P&Ms' first royal duty was more recent – in 1928 for Edward, Prince of Wales (later Edward VIII), on a visit to Armoury House. Their first really significant duty was in April 1948 when King George VI and Queen Elizabeth attended a service at St Paul's Cathedral to mark their silver wedding anniversary.

In the spirit of austerity, the guard of honour, provided by the HAC Regiment, was in battledress khaki. But to make the event more colourful, the City Lieutenancy had borrowed some Yeomen Warders from the Tower of London to line the cathedral steps, ranged a line of gold-clad State Trumpeters along the arcade at the top, and placed the red-coated Pikemen to hold the ground at the bottom where, in

1940, JB's bomb squad had dug out the big bomb from under the west front of the cathedral.

The royal party drove over from Buckingham Palace in open-top landaus at a fast trot with a Household Cavalry escort. As the Queen entered the west churchyard she was charmed by the low bow made to her by the P&M captain. Behind her, a cavalry charger eyed up the captain's lobster pot helmet and strangely shaped leading staff, gave a shrill whinny and bolted back down Ludgate Hill.

Archbishop Geoffrey Fisher took, as the subject of his sermon, the importance of the family.

> Within the natural order God ordained marriage, the home, and the family, and universally among mankind, men, women, children have found in the home among their household gods the central point of their personal and social lives, the focus of their natural instincts and affections, the basis of such security of soul as they may have attained.

With all its flaws, continued Fisher, the family remains the basic survival unit of human society. A healthy, well-functioning society should operate as a family lived out on a national scale. The Royal Family, a real, living family with a unique role, symbolises both the basic family unit and this extended national family.

Chapter Eight

1950–1953
Soldiering On

Cold War

In June 1950, the Pikemen and Musketeers appeared for the first time at the Royal Tournament at Earl's Court – a major exercise where the Company provided a sixty-three-strong display team at two performances a day for three weeks.

The display was almost entirely Pikemen supplemented by ten to twelve Musketeers. A shortage both of muskets and Musketeers had reduced the Musket Division to a shadow of its pre-war glory. Horace Pothecary, who had spent his entire career avoiding any form of promotion, was almost the only person left who understood the complicated musket drills and as such was compelled to accept the post of serjeant of muskets. The Musketeers did, however, retain an element of their pre-war jauntiness by continuing to wear their long, seventeenth-century-style wigs.

And there were other challenges. The crowded changing areas buzzed like a wasps' nest, and extreme vigilance was required. A Pikeman might, with only moderate risk, leave his sash and gauntlets for five minutes, but if he so much as stooped to adjust his knee ties, it was reasonably certain that afterwards he would seek in vain his pike, his sword and every item of his armour.

The day after the final performance, North Korea, with Stalin's blessing, invaded South Korea. Once again, Stalin thought the West would not intervene, and once again, he was wrong. By autumn, an American-led alliance had pushed the North Koreans back across the 38th parallel into North Korea and beyond. At this point China intervened, pouring troops over the border; the war escalated and America found itself on the back foot, with President Truman stating publicly that the use of nuclear weapons was 'under active consideration'.

Britons worried that, with America fully engaged in Korea, Europe was wide open to Soviet incursion. All the old fears of air attack returned, much worse now that Stalin had the atom bomb. There was a rush to revive Britain's air defences and a call for volunteers. The November Lord Mayor's Show took 'Civil Defence' as its theme, with displays by the City Specials and the volunteer fire, ambulance and rescue services. The fire brigade volunteers extended two fire escape ladders to form an arch over the procession as it entered St Paul's churchyard. The spectacle was covered by Pathé News, with the commentator invoking the spirit of the Blitz:

> Tableau after tableau hammers home the need for recruits for all the Civil Defence services. Peace has indeed been dearly bought in two world wars. Let us work to keep that peace now and, in so doing – we shall remember them.

Most P&Ms did their civil defence with the Specials, but Pikeman Major R.A.D. Butler, a veteran of the Burma campaign, took leave of absence from the Bank of England to fight in Korea, and Pikeman Colonel J.B., now in his seventies, put on uniform one last time to command one of the newly revived Home Guard units (8th Surrey Battalion, Reigate Company).

Time passed. The Korean War settled into a stalemate and Stalin did not invade Europe. In October 1951, the UN met in London for UN week. At Guildhall, with the Pikes in attendance, Lord Mayor Sir Denys Lowson expressed his continued faith in the UN:

> The golden ages of man have been those periods when some strong unity of nations existed. The United Nations charter has been founded on the need for peace and security. It embraces the whole world. Let us make it a lasting reality.

Marshal of the RAF Sir John Slessor was less sanguine:

> The next twenty years will almost inevitably decide whether the world is to go forward, to conditions far better than ever dreamt of by our forebears, or backward to a darker age than ever known.

That same month, Churchill won the general election. At his first Lord Mayor's Banquet as prime minister, he inspected a guard of honour of Pikemen in Guildhall Yard and entered the Old Library to a fanfare and standing ovation. During the election, he had been criticised as a warmonger and he now took a conciliatory line, using a metaphor based on the Guildhall statues of Gog and Magog – destroyed in the Blitz but soon to be restored. In City legend, they were manifestations of opposing elemental forces harnessed by the City as guardians of its peace and prosperity. In Churchill's speech, the two warring giants became the two opposing ideologies of world politics. Both, he said, were made up of warm-hearted human beings who 'wanted only to do their best for their country, their neighbours and themselves' but were beset by ideologues seeking to force them into conflict with each other. It was up to the Lord Mayor, the City, and everyone with a concern for world affairs, to use 'ordinary common-sense to keep Gog and Magog from colliding and smashing each other to atoms'.

Military

In the late 1940s, the Company had been increasingly called on to support the military at army reviews and inspections. As the political situation began to stabilise, the bookings shifted towards more civilian-friendly events such as the 1950 Royal Tournament, followed in 1951 by the first post-war Searchlight Tattoo at West Ham and in 1952, the White City Tattoo. At White City the final display – Attack from the Skies! – contained two distinct elements. One, echoing the Wimbledon display of 1939, demonstrated the response of a TA anti-aircraft convoy to an air attack, with hostile planes picked up by searchlights and AA guns coming into action to shoot them down. The other picked up on the new Cold War spy genre, with an enemy agent landing by parachute to steal secret radar equipment, being spotted and chased round the arena, and finally escaping by helicopter.

The P&Ms also appeared in the revived Woolwich Tattoo, at the fiftieth anniversary of the foundation of the Territorial Army, as bodyguard to Viscount Alanbrooke in his role as Master Gunner of St James's Park (the ceremonial head of the Royal Artillery) and at the Festival of Remembrance at the Albert Hall, where, after their usual drill display, they joined the ranks of servicemen and women in the arena for the memorial service, with clouds of poppies falling silently around them.

In 1951, the whole nation was uplifted by the Festival of Britain, a celebration of British design and technology. The P&Ms again held the ground for the grand opening ceremony at St Paul's, where the

King spoke of the festival as 'a symbol of Britain's abiding courage and vitality'.

Other events were still subject to austerity controls. In 1951, the incoming Lord Mayor was told that he could not have a theme for his show. This reduced the length of the procession from 1½ miles to half a mile and the cost by something or other. The *Sussex Daily News* described what was left of the show as 'the dullest for very many years … the Pikemen were colourful, otherwise there were merely detachments of forces to look at.'

Nineteen fifty-one was also the year when the Lord Mayor's coach was finally fitted with a mechanical brake, consisting of a metal wheel that locked on to the rear wheels, albeit still applied by a man walking behind the coach. The Pikemen rejoiced.

> Sing muses with uplifted voice
> The progress of Sir Leslie Boyce
> Whose coach with a new-fangled brake
> Down Ludgate Hill its course did take
> Without as in preceding years
> Impinging on the wheelers' rears
> Or buffeting with startling bumps
> Their mute and uncomplaining rumps.

In 1952, Parliament, still keen to reduce expenditure, approved a new fixed route for the show, reducing the distance from 7 to 5 miles. The tour through the Lord Mayor's ward was abolished and, on leaving the Law Courts, the procession no longer continued to Trafalgar Square but turned left down Arundel Street into Temple Place and back along the Embankment.

As for the streets through which they marched, Gresham Street and Cheapside were still in ruins. All that was left of Wax Chandlers' Hall was a rusticated wall; Haberdashers' a ruined doorway. Mercers' and Saddlers' were in a similar state. The stone walls and towers of St Lawrence Jewry, St Mary-le-Bow and St Vedast's were still standing, but the roofs were gone and the interiors gutted.

As the procession entered St Paul's churchyard the sense of devastation became overwhelming. Everything to the north – Greyfriars, Paternoster Row, the Barbican – was gone. The east side was a mass of rubble; the stump of a single tower in its middle was all that was left of St Augustine's, where Faith the cat had won her bravery award in 1940. On Ludgate Hill, the buildings on either side had been bombed down to their basements, leaving the road a narrow causeway with 15-foot drops on either side.

Royal

The P&Ms first met the 23-year-old Princess Elizabeth in March 1950 at a Mansion House dinner. At the age of 25, she became queen. The proclamation in state to announce her coronation was scheduled for 7 June 1952. The HAC Regiment should have provided its usual guard of honour at the Royal Exchange but, in June, it would be on annual camp. The City's Royal Marine Reserves replaced the HAC on 4 June at a state visit by the prime minster of Australia, and could have done the same on 7 June. Instead, the City Lieutenancy took the then unusual step of asking the P&Ms to substitute for an active military unit. They duly paraded at the Royal Exchange, out for the first time under the orders of the GOC London District, the regular army commander of the London Garrison.

1. 1639 frontispiece of Barriffe's *the yong artilleryman*: portrait of William Barriffe opposite the HAC coat of arms with a contemporary pikeman and musketeer as supporters.

2. *The Man in Brass*: The Lord Mayor's Show, 1844. (See p. 118.)

3. The Halberdiers: HAC assault-at-arms, March 1890.

4. Postures of the pike: HAC sports day, July 1925.

5. Changing room, 1925.

6. Musketeers 'Give fire!' for the first time, July 1930.

7. The Lord Mayor's Show, November 1936.

8. Commercial Street Specials, September 1940. Seated: Pothecary (second from left); Bright (second from right).

9. Churchill, accompanied by Lieutenant Colonel John Bamford Smith, inspects the Docks Garrison, late 1940.

10. P&Ms on television: Alexandra Palace, November 1947.

11. The Lord Mayor's Show, November 1950. The tower of St Augustine's is visible among the ruins in front of St Paul's. Fire brigade volunteers have extended two escape ladders to form an arch over the procession with the City flag at its apex.

12. Drumbeater Ayers, 1925.

13. Pothecary explains the postures of the musket, 1950.

14. Goold Walker in pre-war Royal Artillery full dress.

15. Muzzle-loading muskets, 1963.

16. The Company at the Royal Tournament, July 1950 – a rascally looking lot!

17. Escort to the beef: Royal Society of St George, April 1952. Drumbeater Ayers to the fore.

18. Churchill inspects a Pike guard of honour: Guildhall, June 1955.

19. The Queen presents the Company with her Royal Warrant: July 1955.

20. Thirteen years after the war, Ludgate Hill is still a precarious causeway, with deep bomb sites on either side. The Lord Mayor's Show, 1958.

21. The Lord Mayor's Easter Banquet: Mansion House, 1959.

22. P&Ms marching down the new London Wall, 1963.

23. Whitbread's cellar, 1966. Left to right in P&M uniform: Fish, Bonser, Champness, Rhodes and Pryke.

24. JAK cartoon: *Evening Standard*, 1972. The Queen visited the City and the site of the Barbican Centre for her silver wedding anniversary. Engelbert Humperdinck's 1967 hit 'The Last Waltz' was a regular at anniversaries.

25. Opening of New London Bridge, March 1973.

26. P&Ms in Berlin, 1973. The Berlin Wall can be seen running along the bottom of the Brandenburg Gate.

27. Whitbread's naming ceremony for Pikeman and Musketeer at the Artillery Ground, 1973.

28. Elder Drumbeater Ayers in 1960.

29. Royal Artillery Massed Bands: programme cover, 1986.

30. Escorting Charles I to his execution: Royal Military Tattoo, 2000.

31. An Alpini veteran displays a cake showing the flags of Italy and England: Vittorio Veneto, November 2018.

32. Wet weather wear – Jacobean overcoats: Guildhall, 1951.

33. Wet weather wear, 2015 – guards' capes, with the City colours overhead.

The coronation itself, on 2 June 1953, was a national event, with the Company's role limited to escorting the Lord Mayor's coach to the west door of Westminster Abbey. The City's main coronation celebration came in July with a waterborne version of the Lord Mayor's Show: a flotilla of 149 vessels sailing from Greenwich to the newly built Festival Hall on Bankside, where the Queen took the salute. The City had asked the HAC to participate, but the regiment was again busy and so, for a second time, the P&Ms substituted.

The flotilla portrayed four themes: Her Majesty's Services; Industry and Commerce; River and Marine Services; and Historical Tableaux. There was a Civil Defence display, with two Civil Defence boats communicating with each other by state-of-the-art walkie-talkies, and a third with a giant, animated puppet of a Civil Defence air raid officer. The Pikemen were distributed among the Historic Tableaux barges, and when it rained it was noted that they stepped smartly back under the nearest awning to preserve their shiny armour.

The P&Ms also provided a guard of honour for the Royal Society of St George's Coronation Banquet, held at the Savoy with over 400 attendees. Dinner was announced by a fanfare of State Trumpeters. Red, white and blue candles in silver candelabra and menu cards tied with red and white ribbons decorated the tables, a large St George's banner hung floodlit behind the president's chair and flags of the Commonwealth were dotted around the room. The guest of honour, HRH Princess Alice, Countess of Athlone, and the president of the Society, Field Marshal Montgomery, were escorted by HAC Pikemen and Yeomen Warders.

With rationing still in force, much of the food was contributed by overseas branches of the Society. The salmon came from the Fisheries Association of British Columbia, the barons of beef from the Society in Queensland, Australia, the pudding and fruitcake from Sydney,

Australia, the rum from the West Indies, the cheese from Ontario, Canada, the wines from South Africa, the soft drinks from Southern Rhodesia, and the coffee from Kenya. Grace was said by the Bishop of London and sung by a quartet from the Guildhall School of Music and Drama.

Churchill

The Company's pre-war duties at Armoury House were also beginning to resume. The first post-war Mess Club Dinner was held in 1948:

> Full fifty Paces from the changing room
> The Pikemen marched (or shuffled) through the Gloom
> To line the Staircase and obstruct the Way
> Upon the evening of St Mothball's Day
> Intent great MILTON's line to illustrate
> 'They also serve who only stand and wait.'

Then, in 1953, the HAC held its first post-war St George's Day dinner. Edward Heath, recently elected MP for Bexley and Churchill's chief whip, had arranged for the prime minister to attend as the principal guest. At the appointed time (7.30 pm) the Pikes lined up to receive them. But no one arrived. There had been a political crisis and Churchill had decided that he would have to stay in Parliament waiting for a critical late-night vote.

But at 7.45 pm, Churchill miraculously appeared. Heath had assured him that the dinner would be over by 10.30 pm and he would not be needed in the House until 2 am. As he came into the entrance hall, the shout went up from the Elder Serjeant: 'Have a care!' and the stamp of the Pikemen's feet was heard in the long room above. The prime minister ascended the staircase and at the top, Heath recalled, 'The doors of the great hall were flung open. Everyone seated at dinner immediately rose to their feet and cheered him loudly all the way around the place.'

After dinner, Churchill gave a speech. Stalin had died two months earlier, and there was fresh hope for world peace. But Churchill no longer saw the UN as the way forward. Intended as an international forum for cooperation between nations, it had instead become a supra-national bureaucracy. He said:

> If St George wanted to rescue a maiden from being eaten by a dragon nowadays, he could not simply ride in and rescue her. The UN would preside, intermediate, propose a conference with the Dragon, lend the Dragon a lot of money and refer the maiden's release to Geneva or New York, with the Dragon reserving all rights.

Churchill's main message was that we must not relax just because Stalin was dead. Communism and democracy were still fundamentally opposed to each other, and if the West accepted communism as morally equivalent to democracy, the West would fail.

> While foreign nations grow ever more aggressive, we remain paralysed by our theoretical doctrines … Nothing can save England if she will not save herself. If we lose faith in ourselves, in our capacity to guide and govern, if we lose our will to live, then indeed our story is told.

At 10 pm, the 79-year-old prime minister went back to the House for his 2 am vote.

Chapter Nine

1954–1959
Recovery

In the second half of the 1950s, Britain began to recover. Rationing finally ended in 1954, with meat, the last rationed food staple, deregulated in July.

November 1954 saw the return of a special theme for the Lord Mayor's Show. This was 'The Colonies Come to Town!' featuring displays from all over the Commonwealth and was hugely popular. The *Sheffield Telegraph* wrote:

> Londoners were delighted to see the return of the tableaux and the pageantry. ... There was a cheer for everyone in the two-mile procession, but a crowd must have its favourites, and the cheering mounted for the girls in Cypriot native costume, and the West Indian calypso band.

In 1954, the Lord Mayor moved his saluting base from the entrance to Guildhall Yard to the more spacious crossing at Mansion House, where a temporary balcony was erected, on which he now took the salute.

In 1959, the date of the Lord Mayor's Show was changed by an Act of Parliament from 9 November to the second Saturday in November, ending the disruption of weekday traffic and making it easier for spectators to attend.

Government restrictions on commercial building were also coming to an end. At the November 1953 Lord Mayor's Banquet, a jovial Churchill told his audience: 'Tomorrow we are abolishing [building] licences and leaving you to a large extent to be the judges of your own affairs.' A wave of new building followed. Among the first to benefit was the Guildhall itself, with a new stone-vaulted roof, new stained-glass windows, chandeliers and panelling. The statues were mended and cleaned and a gallery erected with new statues of Gog and Magog.

In December 1956, the P&Ms guarded the Queen when she opened a new extension to the Baltic Exchange. At this time, the fixed sterling–dollar exchange rate meant that the foreign currency generated by the Baltic was particularly valuable to Britain's balance of payments, and the Queen praised the Exchange's position as an international centre for shipping and marketing of grain and oilseeds, where everyday business worth millions of pounds was carried out by word of mouth alone.

Civic

The communal spirit and collective purpose of the war years was still in everyone's minds. Lord Alanbrooke, sponsoring the 1947 HAC recruiting drive, spoke of the wonderful spirit of cooperation of the war years. Churchill, at his first post-war Lord Mayor's Banquet, described Guildhall's war-scarred interior and battered monuments as reminders of the supreme ordeal of 1940, which 'we all endured and won together'.

And everyone wanted that spirit to continue. In the City, it led to a revival of interest in City history, institutions and customs, with the P&Ms increasingly called on, partly for their decorative appearance, partly because of their now official role as the Lord Mayor's bodyguard, and partly as a visual evocation of City identity and history.

The Company had provided a guard of honour for the Lord Mayor's Banquet (guest speaker, the prime minister) since 1927. In the second half of the 1950s, it began to provide guards for other civic events, beginning with the annual dinner for the Masters and Prime Wardens of the Livery Companies (1956), then the Bankers and Merchants Dinner (1957, guest speaker the Chancellor of the Exchequer), then the Court of Aldermen, the Court of Common Council, the judges, and the archbishops and bishops (all 1958), and the Easter Banquet (1959, guest speaker, the Foreign Secretary).

Most of these new events took place at Mansion House, where the Pikemen formed a corridor through which guests passed to be received by the Lord Mayor with (standing behind him) a personal guard comprising an ensign (junior officer) carrying the Company standard, a Drumbeater and two Pikemen. When the reception finished, the escort conducted the Lord Mayor and his principal guests to their seats in the Egyptian Room.[7]

Guildhall events were larger and grander, with anything up to 800 guests. Here the duty might begin with the Pikes forming a guard of honour in Guildhall Yard, followed by guard duty on the stairs and reception areas in the Art Gallery, Print Room and Old Library, and finally escorting the principal guests to the dais in the Great Hall.

The Pikes were also paraded now for visits by civic and overseas dignitaries. Here, proper ceremony was essential to mark the significance of the event and avoid looking cheap. Full state visits typically began with a guard of honour on Horse Guards Parade provided by the Foot Guards, followed by a state banquet at Buckingham Palace with the Yeomen of the Guard lining the

----

7. The main Georgian dining hall designed in a Grecian style, considered in the eighteenth century an Egyptian style.

corridors. Often this was followed (the 1946 UN visit providing a good precedent) by a second state banquet at Guildhall, where the visiting head of state was welcomed by the Lord Mayor in the name of British trade and commerce. Here the HAC Regiment provided the guard of honour in Guildhall Yard, while the Pikes took the 'Yeomen of the Guard' role inside. The first visit of the new reign was the King of Sweden in June 1954, followed by (among others) Emperor Haile Selassie of Ethiopia (October 1954), King Faisal of Iraq (July 1956) and the Shah of Iran (April 1959).

The post-war enthusiasm for history and community also saw a revival of interest in the historic City livery companies. The earliest recorded appearance of the P&Ms at a livery event was the Gold and Silver Wyre Drawers in 1938, followed by the Founders in 1947, the Fan Makers in 1954 (a duty that still continues), the Gardeners in 1957 and the Fruiterers in 1958.

Royal

The Pikes continued to parade for the Royal Family when they visited the City, beginning in May 1954 with the new queen's first post-coronation visit (a dry run for the King of Sweden's state visit a month later).

In July 1955, the P&Ms were formally brought into the military command structure when, at Armoury House, the Queen presented the Company with her Royal Warrant. The tone of this short document (the HAC had been served with a similar one in 1863, when it was told that it would no longer be permitted to appoint its own officers) is that a vigorous but potentially unreliable organisation is to be harnessed in the service of the state (shades of Gog and Magog).

> A body … styled the company of Pikemen and Musketeers.
> have attended as part of the Military parade on great occasions
> of State and other ceremonial occasions and… it is expedient
> to regulate them by authorising the occasions on which they
> can parade and limit their numbers.

Henceforth, the P&Ms might only parade on public occasions when summoned by the GOC London District or the Lord Mayor, in each case with the approval of the HAC's Colonel Commandant (these three now known as 'our three governors').

The warrant did not create anything new. It acknowledged and shaped something that already existed. The Company of Pikemen and Musketeers was now recognised as a ceremonial unit of the British Army, entitled to wear British service medals on their uniforms and to carry the red cross of St George as their company standard.

Churchill

In June 1953, Churchill had a stroke, and was expected to retire soon. In anticipation of this his fellow MPs clubbed together to have his portrait painted by Graham Sutherland, the City commissioned Oscar Nemon to sculpt a bronze statue, and Lord Beaverbrook paid Hammond & Champness, a firm of lift specialists, to install a stair lift at Chartwell.

Hammond & Champness's sales director was Pikeman Colonel Geoffrey Champness, a Second World War veteran who had joined the Pikes four years earlier. On arrival at Chartwell, he was met by Churchill, followed by a butler bearing a large whisky and a 'simply enormous cigar'. Churchill's first words were: 'I hope you drink and I hope you smoke!' Champness said he did and they sat down and chatted. Churchill finally asked him why he was there and was deeply offended by the answer, saying he was not decrepit enough to need a lift. At this point Mrs Churchill arrived and asked where the lift was going. Churchill looked at his feet and Mrs Churchill said, 'Winston, you go back to your office, and I will deal with Mr Champness.' The site for the lift was settled within the next ten minutes.

In November 1954, on Churchill's eightieth birthday, the Sutherland painting was unveiled in Westminster Hall. Churchill was horrified. He thought, with some justification, that Sutherland had painted him as a senile old man who had had a stroke. He was far happier with the City's bronze. Arriving at Guildhall on 27 June 1955, he was greeted by the P&M captain, inspected a Pikemen guard of honour and entered the Great Hall to unveil the statue, which, he said, was a very good likeness.

Back at Chartwell, the lift was installed but Churchill found it much too slow and his secretary asked Champness if he could provide a faster one. Champness said this would cost much more and take nine months to install. The secretary then told Champness to write to Churchill, explaining the problem in as much technical detail as possible. Churchill began reading the letter, was irritated, then bored, then lost interest and finally told his secretary to write back, thanking Champness for his explanation and the efficient way he had carried out the work.

Cold War

In Russia, the new Soviet leader, General Secretary Nikita Khrushchev, thought that the Cold War had been a serious mistake. In April 1956, accompanied by Marshal Nikolai Bulganin, he made a goodwill visit to Britain. After talks with Prime Minister Anthony Eden in Downing

Street, they travelled to the City for a formal luncheon hosted by the Lord Mayor.

Soviet security entered the Mansion House salon ahead of the main party, saw two lines of men wearing body armour and carrying heavy weapons, and quickly placed a KGB operative with a suspicious bulge under his coat next to each Pikeman. A few minutes later, the main party arrived and the Lord Mayor explained the nature and origins of his bodyguard. Marshal Bulganin then told the KGB to stand down and showed a genuine interest in the Pikemen's role and turnout.

The luncheon menu steered a fine line between respecting the importance of the guests and not looking too decadent. The main course, roast Scotch beef with horseradish sauce, garden peas and Jersey new potatoes, evoked the hearty English yeoman. The accompanying drinks offered a choice of (for the effete bourgeois) 1949 Louis Roederer champagne, or (for the honest proletarian) 1953 Commonwealth ale or Burton-brewed pale ale.

Afterwards, Marshal Bulganin gave a cautiously positive speech. Clear, sunny weather had prevailed since he and Mr Khrushchev had arrived on Wednesday and he hoped for similar conditions in the world's political weather: 'The improvement of relations between us, the development of our ties and contacts, will be achieved gradually, step by step.'

Khrushchev said something similar when he met the Queen: 'You don't like communism; we don't like capitalism. The only thing left is peaceful coexistence.' This was nowhere near as benign as it sounded. Khrushchev deplored Stalin's aggression, not because he disapproved of it *per se*, but because it had provoked the West into active resistance. Left to itself, the West would sink into decadence and the forces of history – the communist destiny of the world – would engulf them.

Sometimes the forces of history needed a bit of a push. In the autumn of 1956, Khrushchev crushed a populist uprising in Hungary.

The P&Ms passed the hat and made a donation to the Lord Mayor's Hungary Relief Fund.

The next year the Lord Mayor was asked to attend a British trade fair in Finland and bring the P&Ms with him. On 5 September 1957, at 0645 hours, a fifteen-man detachment mustered at the Waterloo Air Terminal for the Company's first overseas trip: coach to Heathrow, then an 0851 hours flight travelling at 340mph, a stop to refuel at Copenhagen and landing at 14.53 hours at Helsinki.

This was no ordinary trade fair. It was a charm offensive, designed to convince Finland – balanced precariously at the northern end of the Iron Curtain – that it should not succumb to Soviet influence. In addition to British manufacturing, it also showcased Britain's cultural and military strengths.

On the cultural side there were orchestras conducted by Sir Arthur Bliss and Sir Malcom Sergeant, a fashion show, a display of British farming techniques, a motor rally, an athletics meeting, and a trade cinema showing a pre-release screening of *The Battle of the River Plate*.

On the military side the Royal Navy sent HMS *Maidstone* and HMS *Ocean*, with a show of naval aircraft and two helicopters providing rescue demonstrations, while RAF Hawker Hunter jets gave aerial displays in the skies overhead.

The procession for the official opening was led by a detachment of Finnish mounted police, followed by a Royal Marines band, the pipes and drums of the Argyll and Sutherland Highlanders, marching detachments of Royal Marines and sailors from HMS *Ocean* and *Maidstone*, as well as industrial floats displaying British goods. At the back came a detachment of City Specials, the City Aldermen, and finally the Lord Mayor's coach with his Pikemen marching alongside.

The visit was a success and Finland remained culturally part of the West and politically neutral to the end of the Cold War.

Chapter Ten

1960s–1970s
The Affluent Society

Affluence

As the 1960s dawned, Britain was becoming more affluent – with more money to spend, more things to buy. One of the must-haves was a television, providing a new window on the world and, occasionally, on the Pikemen and Musketeers. The BBC began its television coverage of the Lord Mayor's Show in 1946, and the Lord Mayor's Banquet in 1953. In 1958, the P&Ms appeared in BBC coverage of the Festival of Remembrance at the Albert Hall. In 1959, the celebrity panellists on the television game show *What's My Line?* failed to guess the profession of their special mystery guest. When the lights went up it was Geoffrey Champness – now the 'Captain of the Lord Mayor's Bodyguard of Pikemen and Musketeers'. In the 1960s, the P&Ms also appeared in Rediffusion television documentaries on the Civil War, and in 1968 in an ITV episode of *The Saint*, where Roger Moore defeated an attempt to assassinate the Lord Mayor during the Lord Mayor's Show when a poisoned dart was fired from one of the floats.

In cinemas the P&Ms continued to appear in Gaumont newsreels and the new *Look at Life* documentaries. They also featured in the educational children's magazine *Look and Learn*, in jigsaws, on Huntley and Palmers biscuit tin lids and as 'cut-out and keep' figures on the back of Kellogg's Corn Flakes packets. In the West End, they provided a ceremonial bodyguard for Princess Alice, Duchess of Gloucester at the 1956 premier of the Hollywood spectacular *The Conqueror* (with a personal appearance by the star of the film, John Wayne himself). They also escorted Princess Alice at a 1968 gala performance of Harry Secombe's musical *The Four Musketeers* and at the 1970 premiere of the Civil War epic *Cromwell*.

In the press, the *Tatler* ran a two-page feature on Ye Feast, showing the Company relaxing in 'soft kit', drinking tankards of mulled ale and smoking churchwarden pipes (both incorporated into the event following the 1936 Huntingdon pageant). In 1966, an *Evening Standard* journalist wrote:

> The climax of Ye Pikemen's dinner was the serving of the most delicious mulled ale I have ever encountered. I asked Musketeer John Brinkman, who made it, for the recipe. This is what he said: 'Heat six pints of barley wine. Add half a bottle of ginger wine, half a pound of demerara sugar, half a pound of clear honey, a quarter tea-spoon each of ground nutmeg, cloves and mace. Finish off with a small pinch of cinnamon and a slice of lemon. Bring almost to the boil and serve. This is enough for 30 generous savings. If you want to get quietly stoned all by yourself you won't need quite so much.'

The P&Ms also stood guard at the Lord Mayor's own media event – the Midsummer Banquet, a celebration of arts and media and a major feature of the London season from 1961 to 1974. Stars of stage and screen passing between the lines of Pikemen included comedians Morecambe and Wise, composer Sir Arthur Bliss, author J.B. Priestley, TV personalities Richard and David Attenborough, comedy song team Flanders and Swann and television magician David Nixon. In 1967, Gina Lollobrigida arrived dressed as Titania. In 1968, Dame Edith Evans was about to give her name to the toastmaster when he said he knew who she was. 'How terribly sweet of you to remember me!' she said.

The P&Ms also did their bit for higher learning, escorting the Lord Mayor in 1971 at the dedication of new City of London Polytechnic and guarding him again in 1976 when he opened the new City University campus and became the university's rector (a post that the incumbent Lord Mayor continues to hold).

The Show

Until 1960 the Lord Mayor's coach was kept in the Greenyard, the old City stables in Whitecross Street. When the new Barbican development made this impractical, Whitbread's, who still used horse-drawn drays to deliver their beer and had been providing heavy horses for the coach since 1955, volunteered to take over its storage as well. On Lord Mayor's Day, the P&Ms' first call was now at Whitbread's eighteenth-century brewery in Chiswell Street to collect the mayoral coach and escort it down to Guildhall. On the way, they passed the rest of the procession forming up on London Wall, a major new thoroughfare with a ground-level traffic corridor and pedestrian walkways overhead punctuated by tower blocks. The P&Ms particularly liked the signs on the footbridges warning that the maximum permitted height was 15 feet 6 inches – clearly designed with Pikemen in mind.

Their next stop was Guildhall Yard, now undergoing a major redesign. The old narrow King Street entrance was opened out into a spacious, stone-flagged courtyard, modelled on the communal layout of a monastery. On the west side was a new concrete and glass library wing in 1960s Gothic, to the south the church of St Lawrence Jewry, to the east the patched up Art Gallery, and to the north the august elevations of Guildhall itself.

On the processional route, visible bomb damage was now much reduced and new buildings were everywhere. Gresham Street and Cheapside favoured the featureless 'white box' style, with Haberdashers' Hall and Mercers' Hall rebuilt as part of modern office blocks. Wax Chandlers' Hall bucked the trend with a 1950s version of Queen Anne Revival (red brick with pale stone facings). The Wren churches of St Lawrence Jewry in Gresham Street and St Mary-le-Bow and St Vedast in Cheapside had been sympathetically restored, and real bells now rang out from their towers as the Lord Mayor passed.

At the end of Cheapside, the procession turned south into New Change, a new street that had been built down the east side of St Paul's. On its west edge the new modernistic St Paul's choir school incorporated the ancient tower of St Augustine's (historic home of Faith the cat). To the east was a new Bank of England extension in the same Queen Anne style as Wax Chandlers' but on a much vaster scale. The spaces between were filled with gardens full of flowers.

At the top of Ludgate Hill, the procession passed a notorious 1960s icon – the elevated concrete plaza and strangely uncoordinated tower blocks of the newly erected Paternoster Square. Going down Ludgate Hill the rebuilding was patchier, with the south side still largely made up of a cleared-up bomb site being used as a car park.

After the show finished, and the Lord Mayor was dropped off at Mansion House, the P&Ms escorted the now empty coach back to Chiswell Street, where Whitbread's invited them in for a particularly fine outmess. Musketeer Andrew Izod remembers a free bar, followed by a film show (during which many tired P&Ms dozed off), followed by a late afternoon buffet 'with white-clothed tables groaning with hams, turkeys and salmon with all the trimmings and wines and port to match, followed by speeches and toasts including enthusiastic thanks to Whitbread's'.

Izod was less enthusiastic about the Company's return march to Armoury House, with everyone somewhat the worse for wear and those who had over-imbibed placed in the centre files supported by outer file comrades. By now, darkness had fallen and there was a real risk of an unwary motorist driving into the back of the column. Izod's concerns were picked up in what must have been the P&Ms' first-ever risk assessment, after which the rear of the column was guarded by the Master Sutler carrying a roadworks lantern.

In 1973, Whitbread's named a new pair of its Shire horses 'Pikeman' and 'Musketeer', and their nameplates were formally fastened to their harnesses at a naming ceremony at Armoury House. (Twenty years later, when the pair retired, a new Pikeman and Musketeer stepped into their places, the naming ceremony taking place this time at Whitbread's hop farm in Kent.)

In 1976, the home of the Lord Mayor's coach moved again, this time from Whitbread's Brewery to the newly opened Museum of London on London Wall, where it remains on permanent display, leaving the museum only to prepare for the next Lord Mayor's Show.

Cold War

The Cold War was still there, though visible mostly in the fashion for spy films – Sean Connery in *Thunderball* or Michael Caine in *The Ipcress File*. In 1967, *The Sun* newspaper described a visit by the new Soviet leader Alexei Kosygin to the City:

> Naturally the Lord Mayor's Body Guard turned out, because you can't tell with these foreign fellers … quite what the Company of Pikemen and Musketeers would have done if SMERSH had started something I can't think. Called loudly for a bobby I shouldn't wonder!

Many in the West had now settled for Khrushchev's 'peaceful coexistence', their feathers only slightly ruffled by the 1968 Soviet invasion of Czechoslovakia. But NATO was still facing off against the armies of the Warsaw Pact, and the British Army of the Rhine was still guarding the Inner German Border. There, in the event of a Soviet invasion, the HAC Regiment's new role (from 1973) was to act as stay-behind observation posts (OPs), similar to the role Tubby Ayers had (accidentally) performed when, as a forward observation officer (FOO), he had won his MC at Passchendaele, but with much bigger guns.

The P&Ms continued to make their own small contribution to the stiffening of Western resolve, parading in 1958 for the first state visit by the new president of West Germany (also the first German state visit to Great Britain since 1907). They also stood guard for NATO's twentieth anniversary and at meetings of CENTO and SEATO (versions of NATO covering the Middle East and Southeast Asia respectively).

In 1973, the Company visited the Cold War front line in Berlin. Here the British garrison, deep inside communist territory, held a regular military tattoo to show that, as far as they were concerned, everything was 'business as usual'. The P&Ms were flown out on military transport, took part in a section called 'London Scenes', and gave a display. The volley fire from the Musketeers ended with an unexpected shower of chicken feathers fluttering down from the ceiling and the audience roared with laughter. The presiding general was furious but never managed to find out who was responsible. Afterwards, the P&Ms were given a tour of West Berlin and a visit to the Berlin Wall, where they were photographed in full dress in front of the Brandenburg Gate.

Nineteen seventy-eight saw the P&Ms parading for the first visit by a Warsaw Pact head of state. The president of Romania, Nicolae Ceaușescu, was about to sign a £300 million contract to buy British aircraft, when he announced that he wanted a full state visit and his wife Elena would accept an academic distinction of some sort. The Foreign Office leant on Buckingham Palace, a London polytechnic was found that would give Elena an honorary professorship, and the visit took place. The Ceaușescus were difficult guests and the Queen suffered particularly. The P&Ms' experience was limited to the reception at Guildhall when, at the City banquet in their honour, the Ceaușescus refused to enter the Great Hall while grace was being said, remaining in the Old Library until the Lord Mayor, with an escort of P&Ms, returned to collect them.

Abroad

The P&Ms' role continued to grow and with it the need for professionalism. Geoffrey Champness (captain 1957–61), presiding over a steady expansion of the Company's civic duties, began to improve efficiency and turnout. Richard Vergette (captain 1961–65) wrote the Company's first proper drill book, brought its drill up to regular army standards, and restored the Muskets to their pre-war strength so that, at the 1963 Lord Mayor's Show, for the first time since 1936 it was able to field two full musket divisions marching ahead of and behind the main pike body. At the same show, fifty-three out of a total of fifty-six P&M members were on parade, the youngest being 32, the oldest rising 81.

The City was changing as well. During the 1960s, the London Docks were in terminal decline and commodities and exports gave way to banking and insurance. By the 1970s, the City was becoming a leading international financial centre, with the Lord Mayor increasingly acting as City trade ambassador. At its grandest, this involved his ceremonial bodyguard accompanying him on overseas goodwill visits. The Helsinki British Trade Fair was followed by Zurich (1963), Oslo (1966) and Brussels (1967).

On a second visit to Switzerland in 1970, the Company performed an elaborate series of manoeuvres worthy of Barriffe himself, beginning by greeting the Lord Mayor on his arrival at Zurich Airport, escorting him in a miniature Lord Mayor's Show at Regensberg (led by the City Marshal on horseback accompanied by Kyburg horsemen in hunting pink and fanfares of hunting horns), seeing him off as he left Regensberg by train and then rushing ahead to greet him on his arrival at Lausanne. They performed a similar manoeuvre when he left Ouchy and crossed Lake Geneva on a police launch to land at Lutry. Finally, they accompanied him in a second miniature Lord Mayor's Show in Zurich, marching alongside the Zurich city guilds.

In September 1971, the P&Ms flew to San Francisco to escort HRH Princess Alexandra of Kent at the opening ceremony for British Week. This was followed by five days of duties: displays in a sports arena, as a curtain-raiser at a soccer match, at a Battle of Britain memorial service, and at lunches, dinners and garden parties. There were also fashion shows, an opera, and HMS *Blake*, a helicopter cruiser that had sailed through the Panama Canal to anchor in San Francisco Bay.

In October 1971, they were in Arizona for the opening of London Bridge, recently transported stone by stone to its new home astride the warm waters of Lake Havasu. During the 1960s, the City had discovered that the bridge was, once again, falling down. To pay for the rebuilding cost the City sold the fabric of the bridge to Robert P. McCulloch, an American real estate tycoon, who reconstructed it as the centrepiece of his new retirement home development in Arizona.

For the opening ceremony, the Lord Mayor arrived by barge on the Havasu River, where he was met on landing by a guard of Pikemen who escorted him onto the bridge itself. Here he cut the ribbon, a salute was fired, 5,000 white pigeons and 50,000 balloons were let loose, aeroplanes performed acrobatics overhead, parachutists dropped through the balloons and several more planes wrote messages of welcome in their vapour trails. This was followed by an American version of the Lord Mayor's Show with drum majorettes, cowboys spinning lariats, a Native American band, and a pageant showing the history of London Bridge. At the rear came the City Marshal, in tropical uniform riding on a diminutive pony, and behind him the Lord Mayor's cabriolet, its wheels sinking to their axles in the desert sand, guarded and, at times, pushed by his trusty Pikemen.

McCullough's extraordinary gamble paid off. His costs were more than offset by the publicity generated by the event and applications from retirees flooded in.

In November 1972, the P&Ms paraded at Guildhall to celebrate Her Majesty's silver wedding. Afterwards they provided a second guard in Basinghall Street as the Queen and Prince Philip took an informal walkabout in the construction site that would one day become the Barbican Arts Centre.

On the Thames, a new London Bridge was arising on the foundations of the old, and in March 1973 it was opened by the Queen. The P&Ms were on duty at the north end and on the stairs down to the quayside, an HAC gun battery fired a salute at the Tower of London, church bells rang and crowds cheered. The Queen was accompanied by Edward Heath, who had been her prime minister since 1970. A notorious workaholic, his affection for the HAC was one of his few indulgences – perhaps the only place where he came close to relaxing. He regularly attended reunions and dinners and at City events always stopped to speak to old comrades in the P&Ms. In 1972 at a state banquet for the King of Afghanistan, he enjoyed the looks of puzzlement on the faces of two Afghan generals as he waved his hand at the Pikemen and announced, 'These chaps are members of my regiment – the oldest in the British Army.'

Heath was a notorious Europhile and determined, now that he was prime minister, to take Great Britain into the European Economic Community (EEC). The City had picked up on this in 1971 when the theme of the Lord Mayor's Show was 'The City Serves the Nation', with the emphasis on the opportunities and challenges of Britain's entry into Europe. The 1972 show ran a similar theme, 'The World is Our Market', just around the time Heath was signing on the dotted line, and in January 1973, the UK became part of the EEC.

At this time EEC membership was seen as entirely positive. In January 1973, the P&Ms stood guard at a Guildhall banquet for thirty visiting EEC mayors and municipal delegates who were being shown the financial resources and expertise London could offer. In September 1973, the P&Ms travelled to Brussels to take part in Europalia, an annual celebration of EEC culture and achievements, which that year was showcasing British culture – artwork by David Hockney, singing by Shirley Bassey and music by the Royal Philharmonic Orchestra. The P&Ms guarded the Lord Mayor at a civic reception at the Hotel de Ville and appeared in a British Forces military tattoo. A year later, at the invitation of the local Tastevins, they accompanied the Lord Mayor on a trip to Bordeaux, celebrating Anglo-French friendship.

Members

By now the P&Ms' original Great War veterans were long gone. Frank Bright died in 1949, Goold Walker in 1955 and Poth' in 1957. Tubby Ayers retired in 1966 after forty-one years' service, during which he had risen from the rank of Drumbeater to the fractionally higher rank of Elder Drumbeater.

In their places came a new generation of Second World War veterans. Geoffrey Champness joined the Company in 1949 and became captain in 1957. In the war, he had commanded 86th (HAC) HAA Regiment RA, landing on Juno Beach on D-Day with the Canadian 3rd Division. In the Normandy campaign, his guns had served as anti-aircraft or conventional artillery as the occasion required. Later, in Belgium, with Major Edward Heath as his second in command, he had defended Antwerp and Brussels from V-1 attacks, destroying seventy-eight flying bombs in four and a half months. For this he was awarded an OBE and the Belgian Croix de Guerre (Heath got an MBE).

Jovial Ted Pryke joined the P&Ms in 1958 and served as captain in 1974–77. During his tenure the affluent society declined a notch or two – rampant inflation and a series of strikes and power cuts led to the three-day week, the fall of Heath's government and a top income tax rate of 83 per cent. Pryke was the grandson of Sir William Pryke Bart, Lord Mayor 1925/6 and the first modern Lord Mayor to revive the use of the HAC as his ceremonial escort. In the war, he had served in the Duke of Cornwall's Light Infantry, been captured at Tobruk and held as a PoW in Italy until the Italian surrender in 1943. He escaped from his prison camp just before it was recaptured by the Germans and spent the next thirty-five days walking down the Apennines towards the Allied lines, crossing endless valleys and rivers and hiding from German patrols, initially in hot weather but towards the end in steady rain – a distance of some 500 miles.

Reggie Rhodes joined the P&Ms in 1963 and was captain in 1985–88. In the war, he had served with the Middlesex Regiment in Libya, where he was blown up and severely wounded by an unmarked minefield. Initially considered beyond hope, his life was saved by a New Zealand surgeon who operated on him in a tent during a sandstorm. After a long, slow recovery, he was appointed adjutant on a troop transport that took part in the landings on Sicily and Italy and later transported White Russians to Odessa. Post-war he joined the newly nationalised British Gas and in the 1970s was responsible for the conversion of the whole of the London area to natural gas. He finished his career as deputy chairman of the Southern Gas Board who, on his appointment as P&M captain in 1985, presented him with a silver head for his leading staff.[8]

Other Second World War veterans in the P&Ms at this time included Terry Bonsor – one of the Pikemen on the Huntley and Palmers biscuit tin lid – who had fought in Burma, been wounded and flown out to a field hospital slung under the wing of a light aircraft. John Fish joined in 1963 and served in India with the Essex Regiment, a fairly easy billet but with some nasty experiences during partition. Basil Bonallack, a Royal Artillery FOO like Ayers, won an MC in Sicily when he crossed the Simeto River under heavy machine-gun fire and, when the infantry attack was driven back, remained behind to bring down artillery fire to cover their withdrawal.

---

8. The symbolic badge of office of a seventeenth-century commander. See further page 144.

By the 1970s, the Second World War veterans were being joined by a still younger generation who had done their soldiering after the war. Among them was Pikeman Tom Hearn, who had done his National Service in the Welsh Guards in Berlin, joined the HAC in 1958 and the P&Ms in 1968. It was he who, at the Berlin Tattoo in 1973, persuaded (some might say inveigled) a reckless young Welsh Guardsman to climb up into the roof of the arena to release the feathers just as the muskets fired.

Pikeman Gerald Flint Shipman joined the HAC in 1955 and the P&Ms in 1972. In 1979, he left the P&Ms to found the HAC's second ceremonial unit (so a P&M daughter regiment?). This was the HAC Light Cavalry, a horsed ceremonial unit, recreating a Victorian HAC light cavalry unit that had originally existed between 1861 and 1891, and is still going strong.

Chapter Eleven

1980s
The Winds of Change

The P&Ms' bodyguard role took on a new prominence in May 1986, when Lord Mayor Sir Allan Davis arrived at Heathrow Airport escorted by what United Press International called 'seven burly bodyguards in full armour carrying pikes and muskets'. A month earlier, President Ronald Reagan had bombed terrorist centres in Libya and many Americans had now stopped travelling abroad for fear of reprisals. British Airways' bookings fell by 50 per cent and the Lord Mayor decided to fly to New York to encourage Americans to keep coming to Britain. He told the press: 'I walk in London whenever possible and it seems as safe as it ever was … there is no feeling of oppression that you get in other cities.'

Other P&M appearances were on more conventional lines. Military bookings saw fewer local tattoos and pageants, but more national events – two Musical Pageants at Wembley, a Royal Artillery Massed Bands Spectacular on Horse Guards Parade and an international tattoo at Ghent in Belgium.

In September 1986, the P&Ms appeared for a second time in the Berlin Tattoo. A local reporter described them, with astonishing inaccuracy, as 'thirty pearly kings, the bodyguard of the Mayor of London in their uniforms of 47,000 pearl buttons'.

The P&Ms found Berlin more relaxed than in 1973. This time they not only visited Checkpoint Charlie but also passed through it for a guided tour of East Berlin – long blocks of workers' flats interspersed with Soviet war memorials, as well as the occasional ruined cathedral left as a graphic symbol of the fate in store for the West.

The P&Ms' role at the tattoo was to escort the Lord Mayor in a horse-drawn coach at another miniature Lord Mayor's Show. It soon became clear that the horses had no experience of coach work. At rehearsals, they were so frisky that the Lord Mayor entered the arena on foot. Harnessed up on the first night, they charged in and galloped all over, scattering P&Ms like ninepins. On the second day at the afternoon performance, they were still off at a gallop, but calmed down a bit by the evening performance. Even so, the Pikes had to form up at right angles to the coach and follow it in with weapons shouldered. By the third day the team was being given 100 yards' start before entering the arena and was much more settled as result. And by the fourth and fifth days, everything went perfectly.

Royal

In July 1981, HRH Prince Charles married Lady Diana Spencer in St Paul's Cathedral and the nation celebrated, with the P&Ms putting on a display in Paternoster Square as part of the City's festivities.

In March 1982, the Queen, escorted by the P&Ms, formally opened the Barbican Arts Centre, which she had first visited in November 1972. It had taken ten years to build and was the largest of its kind in Europe, housing the Royal Shakespeare Company, the London Symphony Orchestra and the BBC Symphony Orchestra. The Queen described it as 'a wonder of the modern world'.

A more personal occasion came in May 1987 when the HAC celebrated its 450th anniversary by marching down to Mansion House, where the Queen and Prince Philip took the salute from the balcony.

The regiment then marched to Guildhall, leaving Her Majesty to present the P&Ms with a new colour (the flag of St George). They then provided the Sovereign's Escort from Mansion House to Guildhall, marching alongside her coach in their distinctive 'three and three' formation. Important as this was for the P&Ms, it was a last-minute addition to the programme, designed to give the Lord Mayor and the HAC Regiment time to get back to Guildhall to welcome the Queen's arrival.

The P&Ms were on duty again at Guildhall when the Princess of Wales was presented with her Honorary Freedom of the City. The young princess maintained a very serious face, right up to the moment when the Lord Mayor's Rolls-Royce spluttered and refused to start, when she broke into a shy smile. The motionless ranks of Pikemen were enchanted.

The winds of change blew harder in the last years of the decade. In June 1988, President Reagan, returning from his Moscow summit, stopped off in Guildhall to give a progress report. As the presidential party moved into the main hall, Musketeer Duggie Dugdale claimed that a worried looking US Marine officer hesitated and then deposited his bag, containing the trigger codes for nuclear war, beside the motionless Duggie. Fortunately for World Peace, Duggie did not touch it.

President Reagan, who had been in intense discussions with General Secretary Mikhail Gorbachev, reported that things were looking positive. But he also echoed Churchill's Gog and Magog speech and St George's Day sentiments of thirty years earlier. We must never forget that Soviet dictatorship and Western democracy remain in fundamental opposition to each other. If the West accepted dictatorship as morally equivalent to democracy, the West would fail. 'We have learned the first objective of the adversaries of freedom is to make free nations question their own faith in freedom.'

In March 1989, the P&Ms escorted HRH Princess Alexandra again, this time as guest of honour at a Mansion House fashion show organised by the Lady Mayoress. The duty involved walking up a narrow catwalk from the main salon into the Egyptian Room, at the top of which the Pikemen stayed, balancing precariously, while the opening speeches were made. Later the evening improved when 'some extremely lissom attractive models wearing micro skirts insisted on having their photographs taken with us'. In April, the P&Ms were back at Guildhall for an official 'semi-state' visit by General Secretary Gorbachev. He was met, not by the Queen but by Prime Minister Margaret Thatcher; his guard of honour came, not from the Household Division, but from the RAF, and his visit to the City was not for a state banquet but a speech. Gorbachev echoed Reagan's positive tone of a year earlier. He spoke of a new East–West rapprochement, assured his audience that the USSR was 'building an open, democratic and free society' and invited the Queen to visit Moscow.

In October, the principal guest at Ye Feast was General Patrick Brooking, former GOC British Sector, West Berlin during their 1986 visit. In June 1987, Brooking had been standing beside Reagan at the Brandenburg Gate when the president issued his famous challenge: 'There is one sign the Soviets can make that would be unmistakable … Mr Gorbachev, open this gate! Mr. Gorbachev, tear down this wall!'

At Guildhall back in April, Gorbachev had warned his audience that 'the old [Soviet] ways are still alive and cannot be done away with overnight'. But he was wrong. Less than a month after Ye Feast, on 9 November 1989, huge crowds gathered at the East German side of the wall, demanding its gates be opened. The guards asked for orders but received none. In the end, they simply opened the checkpoints and the people flooded through. The Berlin Wall was gone.

One after another, the Soviet satellites rose against their rulers and swept them aside, mostly bloodlessly. But in Romania, the hated Ceaușescus first put up a fight, then tried to flee and then were captured and shot. On Christmas Day 1989, Romanian television transmitted a video of their dead bodies.

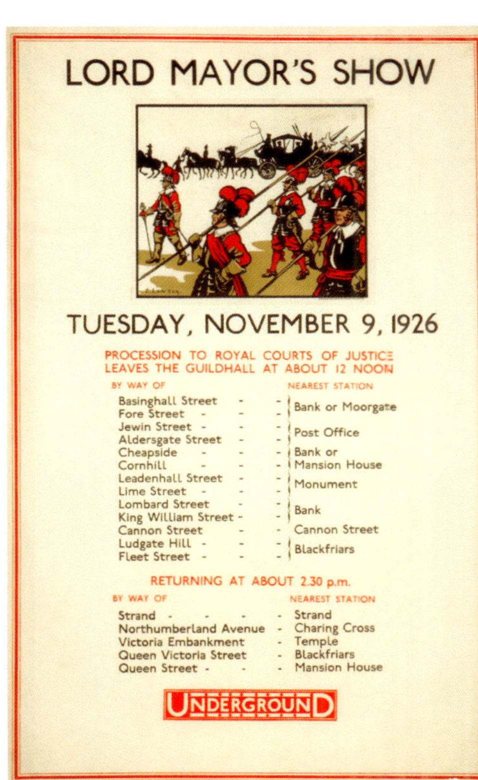

34. The Red Trained Band at Newbury, 1643: Frontispiece *HAC Journal*, 1925.

35. London Transport poster: The Lord Mayor's Show, 1926.

36. Pikemen in Guildhall Yard. Detail from a P&M Christmas card, 1958.

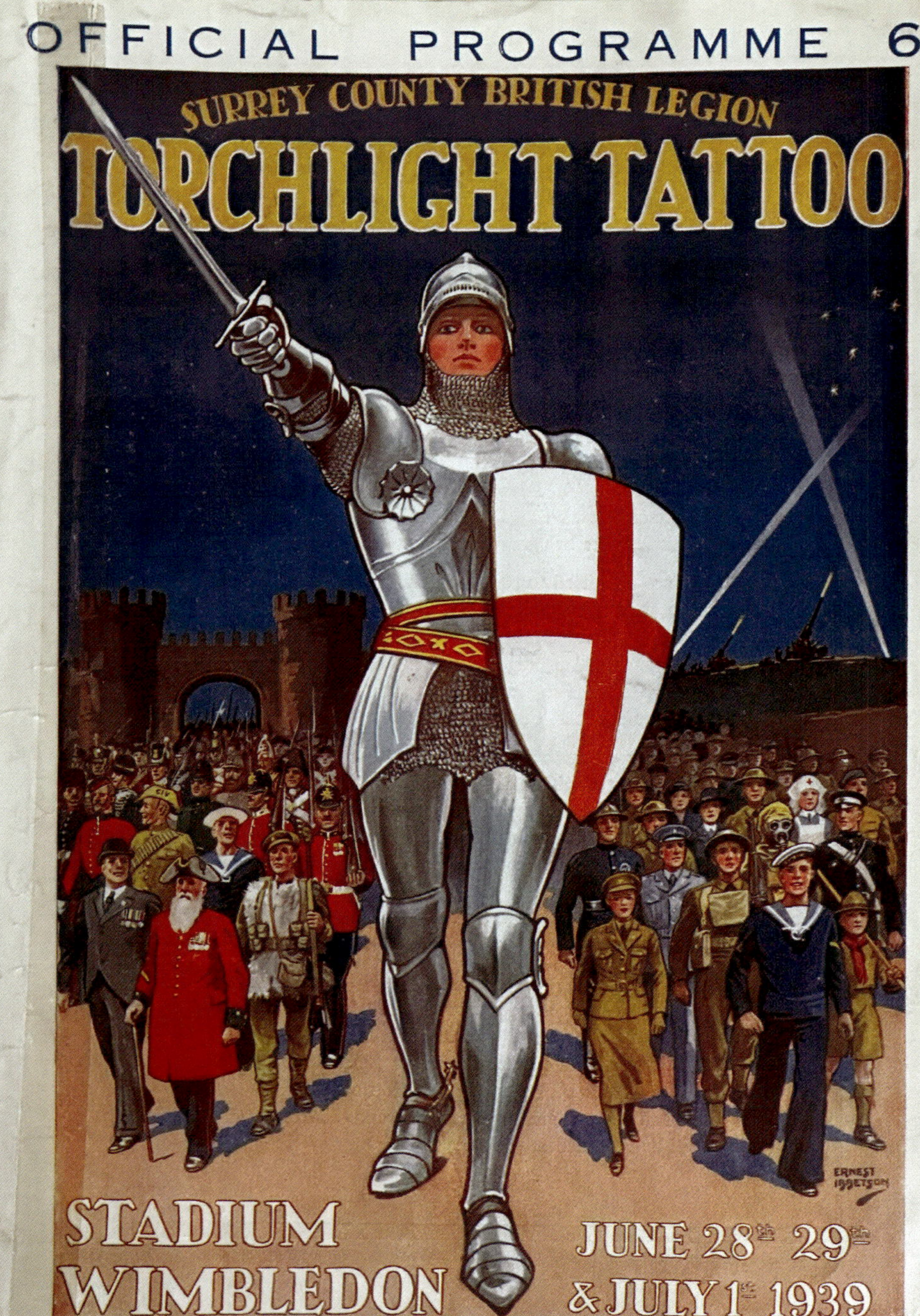

37. England's defenders marching through history: Wimbledon Searchlight Tattoo, June 1939.

38. Pikemen hold the ground at St Paul's: Festival of Britain, 1951.

39. The Pikemen meet the Tiller Girls: Earl's Court, 1992.

40. Lord Mayor Paul Newall reflected in a Pikeman's helmet, November 1993.

41. Give fire breast high!

42. Marching past St Paul's.

43. Festival of Remembrance: Albert Hall, 1998.

44. The Boston 'Ancients' on the march.

45. Lambert & Butler cigarette card: *Interesting Customs & Traditions of the Navy, Army & Air Force*, 1939. The drumbeater is recognisably Percy Ayers.

46. Colonel Farrington as commanding officer of the HAC Infantry Battalion, 1908.

47. The Mayor of Northampton hoisting the Oak Apple wreath onto Charles II's statue.

48. Coach party at the Law Courts.

49. The Captain (David Horn) on Drummond at the start of the 2005 Lord Mayor's Show. Goldsmiths' and Wax Chandlers Halls in the background.

50. P&M Maritime Division: Menorca, 2011.

51. The royal review, 2010. The group photograph.

52. The P&Ms with their chaplain, The Reverend David Reindorp, in 2014, outside the Old State House, Boston.

53. Commemorative postage stamp for the 800th anniversary of the mayoralty in 1989.

54. Vigil for Crown Prince Otto's lying in state: Vienna, 2011.

55. Musketeer Frase with Chelsea Pensioners: The Carmen's Ball, 2015.

56. The Company in Guildhall Yard.

57. The Company at Bruges in 2016 for the 360th anniversary of the Grenadier Guards.

58. Her Majesty and Prince Philip at a Guildhall dinner for Commonwealth High Commissioners in 2016. Prince Philip is about to accost Musketeer Raffety. (See page 96.)

59. Drill display for L'Ordre des Chevaliers Bretvins: Nantes, 2018.

60. Inauguration of Mossbourne Academy Combined Cadet Force, Hackney, at Grocers' Hall, 2019.

Guardians of the City

61. Pikeman, City Trained Bands, 1643. Player's cigarette card: *Uniforms of the Territorial Army*, 1939.

62. Doggett's Waterman and Bargemaster.

63. Statue of Magog in Guildhall.

64. City dragon guarding the entrance to Fleet Street.

65. King Charles III's post-coronation visit to the City: October 2023.

66. Processing the Boar's Head at Armourers' Hall.

67. Guard of honour at the East India Club.

68. The Company at All Saints' Church, Northampton, for Oak Apple Day.

69. Blessing the Company's colours: St Paul's, March 2025.

70. Lady Mayor's guard of honour at Mansion House Crossing: November 2025.

Chapter Twelve

1990s
The End of History

By 1990, the Cold War was over and the Berlin Wall demolished, its fragments sold to tourists as souvenirs. Historian Francis Fukuyama called it 'the end of history'. The great ideological divide – Churchill's Gog versus Magog – was over and Western liberalism was now the only acceptable creed.

In South Africa, the fall of the Berlin Wall spurred the government to end Apartheid and Nelson Mandela went from prison cell to president of the Republic. In 1996, the P&Ms provided him with a guard as he accepted his Honorary Freedom of the City:

> I feel deeply the honour which you have done me. For a community to welcome a person from a faraway land as one of its own, is something that I regard as a very special privilege. It affirms the universality of human experience, and it is eloquent with your care for the well-being of all South Africans. … Let us all join hands in a partnership of peace and prosperity, for all our peoples, for all people everywhere.

Over in the East End, JB's London Docks were being transformed into 'Docklands' – a new financial district for a new generation of global investment banks – a postmodernist city of towers and water and light. The warehouse that, in 1940, had housed JB's HQ company was now the Docklands museum; Rum Quay, which in 1940 had been a conflagration of burning warehouses, was Canary Wharf, with One Canada Square – at 235 metres the tallest building in the UK – at its centre.

EU 1992

On the other side of the English Channel, there was a new Brussels programme of political integration, to be completed on the stroke of midnight on 31 December 1992. The moment when the EEC transformed into the European Union (EU) would be marked by the lighting of a thousand beacons across the twelve EU member states. In the UK the first beacon would be lit by Prime Minister John Major, at a special media event hosted by BBC Radio 1 at Armoury House, with games, music, New Year messages from the worlds of pop and rock, and a fireworks display. The P&Ms lined the entrance hall and great staircase as media celebrities and personalities ascended to the VIP reception in the Long Room. Just before midnight, they assembled again in the entrance hall to escort Major out to light the beacon. But the PM was late, and Big Ben was already chiming when he came rushing down the great staircase and 'shot past us at a considerable pace. We arrived at our appointed positions about half a minute after him and a good two minutes late.'[9]

The event was not a success. Its organisers had expected 5,000–10,000 visitors, but it attracted only 1,000. Evidently, political integration did not have the same pulling power as the old 1970s message of trade and prosperity.

---

9. Taken from a first-person anonymous account in the *HAC Journal*.

Military

The P&Ms continued to appear at the Festival of Remembrance in the Albert Hall when it did not clash with Lord Mayor's Day. Musketeer Paul Champness remembers that the dye from the poppies dropping from the roof stained his somewhat receding hairline with red patches, which led to him later being stopped and examined by the Albert Hall first-aid team.

Other military engagements included the Royal Military School of Music at Kneller Hall (where the Musketeers fired nine volleys during the concert, taking their time from the conductor), appearances at Grenadier Day at Pirbright and at overseas military tattoos at Voorthuizen and Leiden in the Netherlands.

In 1995, the tri-service Beating the Retreat took the Company into the heart of ceremonial London. Assembling at Wellington Barracks they marched up Birdcage Walk and along Whitehall, paused at the Cenotaph to 'Advance pikes!' in tribute to The Fallen. Then a left turn though the archway to be played onto Horse Guards Parade by the band of the Royal Marines. Later the Musketeers again joined in the music, providing small arms fire for Tchaikovsky's *1812 Overture*.

Less pleasantly, the 1990s saw a new series of terrorist bomb attacks, this time aimed directly at the City – June 1990, Armoury House; February 1992, London Bridge Station; and April 1992, the Baltic Exchange, where the P&Ms had guarded the Queen back in 1956. More bombs followed in 1993 in Bishopsgate and 1996 in Aldwych. The City responded with the 'Ring of Steel', channelling traffic into the City through a few carefully controlled entrance points and protective barriers. Now on Lord Mayor's Day, when the P&Ms came marching down Moorgate, they entered a road-narrowing system guarded by a police sentry box and CCTV cameras with number plate recognition.

There was another chicane on Ludgate Hill, while Mansion House and the Law Courts were protected from car bombs by lines of bollards and concrete blocks.

At the procession assembly area on London Wall, the dynamic 1970s' system of walkways and flyovers was gradually being overbuilt by squat, postmodernist tower blocks. Another postmodernist building appeared at No. 1 Poultry – a pink and caramel-striped confection topped by a submarine conning tower and a roof terrace, which, after the beginning of the credit crisis in 2007, became a favourite jumping-off point for City suicides.

Post-modernism did better on Ludgate Hill, where the Thameslink station finally replaced the last City bomb site, together with a series of carefully proportioned, neoclassical office blocks and a small, but perfectly formed, new side street called Pageantmaster Court.

The very last piece of bomb damage to be rebuilt was the Guildhall Art Gallery, whose temporary structure, cobbled together in 1946, had remained in use for the next forty years. In 1985, when rebuilding finally started, the remains of a first-century Roman amphitheatre were discovered under the foundations, causing further delay. Finally, in 1999, the new Art Gallery was finished, its postmodern Gothic counterpointing with the 1970s' Gothic of the Guildhall Library, with the Roman amphitheatre carefully preserved in the basement.

The new Art Gallery was opened in 2000 by the Queen. As they paraded in the foyer of the new building, the P&Ms were pleased to note that the architect had specifically taken account of the need to accommodate their 12-foot pikes. Three years earlier, it had been a different story, when the lowering of the ceiling in the ambulatory corridor had forced the Pikemen, first to attempt to hold their pikes at an angle, and then to vacate the corridor completely in favour of the Musketeers.

Royal

When royalty visits the City the P&Ms are usually out under the orders of the Lord Mayor. But sometimes they provide a royal escort in their own right: 1948 (royal wedding anniversary); 1951 (Festival of Britain); 1971 (San Francisco); and 1987 (Sovereign's Escort).

Another such event came in 1992 when the P&Ms escorted the Prince and Princess of Wales at the Universal Exposition (Expo 92). This was a world's fair celebrating the 500th anniversary of Christopher Columbus's discovery of America, held in Seville over six months, with pavilions representing 100 countries, light shows, restaurants and nightclubs, and 42 million visitors.

Each day was dedicated to a different country and the P&Ms were flown out on military transport for British Day on 21 May. Their part in the opening procession, with temperatures in the 90s, was made tiresome by small boys who 'kept running beside us calling Don Quixote! Don Quixote!' 'Our attempts in Spanish to disperse them failed but "F--- off you little git!" did the trick.' After the royal couple had opened the event, the main body of P&Ms accompanied the royal couple as they toured the commonwealth pavilions while smaller detachments leap-frogged ahead to greet them ('Have a care!') as they arrived at each pavilion. Princess Diana stopped to ask Pikeman David Horn how he kept his medals on his breastplate. 'Personal magnetism Ma'am!' was his reply.[10]

In October, the P&Ms were on duty at Earl's Court for '40 Glorious Years', a national pageant celebrating the fortieth anniversary of the Queen's accession to the throne. It was the biggest indoor production ever staged in Britain, with 4,000 performers, a choir of 500, 2

---

10. Taken from a first-person anonymous account in the *HAC Journal*.

orchestras, and entertainers including Dame Vera Lynn, Petula Clark, Lonnie Donegan, Cliff Richard, Tommy Steele, Cilla Black and Dame Judi Dench.

The P&Ms appeared in the sequence 'London the Capital', marching into the arena with the Guards' bands playing 'They're Changing Guard at Buckingham Palace' and taking up positions along the sides of a vast globe of the world painted on the floor. In a second appearance, they formed an avenue for Anna Massey, portraying Queen Elizabeth I, to pass through and give her Spanish Armada speech:

> I have placed my chiefest strength and safeguard in the loyal hearts and good-will of my subjects; and therefore I am come amongst you … not for my recreation and disport, but being resolved, in the midst and heat of the battle, to live and die amongst you all.

As the P&Ms were waiting to go on, they encountered the Tiller Girls in feathers and sequins. The premier female dance troupe of the 1960s, they had recently re-formed to dance at charitable events. The P&Ms were delighted – 'They had worn very well – better than us!'

Expo '92 was one of the last times the Prince and Princess of Wales appeared in public together and by the end of the year it was known that their marriage was over. The media sided against the Royal Family, even when, on 20 November, fire destroyed a large part of Windsor Castle. Four days later, the Queen attended a Guildhall luncheon, received as usual by the P&Ms. In an unusually personal speech, she said:

> Nineteen ninety-two is not a year on which I shall look back with undiluted pleasure … it has turned out to be an *Annus Horribilis*. … No institution … should expect to be free from

scrutiny. But – we are all part of the same fabric … and that scrutiny … can be just as effective if it is made with a touch of gentleness, good humour and understanding.

Five years later, in November 1997, the P&Ms encountered the Queen at Guildhall again, this time for her golden wedding anniversary. Diana, Princess of Wales had died tragically in August and the press now detected a softening in royal attitudes. Associated Press described Prince Philip's speech as surprisingly personal. 'Tolerance', he said, 'is the one essential ingredient of any marriage; not so important when things are going well, but absolutely vital when things get difficult.'

Chapter Thirteen

Postmodern Military

The new millennium was a new world. The Royal Tournament ended in 1999, replaced in 2000 by a smaller event – the Royal Military Tattoo, which took place on Horse Guards. The P&Ms appeared as part of the historical pageant acting out the origins of the modern British Army – first as Cromwellian troops escorting Charles I to his execution, and returning for the Restoration, when King Charles II, accompanied by his mistress Nell Gwyn, re-entered his kingdom under an avenue of ported P&M pikes.

In 2010 came a second revival – the British Military Tournament – which took place at the old Royal Tournament venue of Earl's Court. The P&Ms played Roundhead foot, levelling their pikes and firing their muskets as Prince Rupert's cavalry (portrayed by the HAC Light Cavalry, in Civil War costumes) circled around them, with the voice of Stephen Fry as Prince Rupert booming over the public address system. The British Military Tournament did well but, in 2013, it too came to an end.

Live events now had to compete with social media and the military resources to support them were no longer there. Regiments had been merged and disbanded, military hospitals closed, buildings sold off, catering outsourced, bands disbanded, and the social capital value of engagement with civilian society increasingly dismissed as an inefficient use of scarce resources.

In this penny-pinching environment, the privately financed P&Ms continued to appear at military events, supported by a combination of booking fees, private and charitable fundraising and (at times) members paying for their own travel and accommodation.

Rome

The commandant of the Guardia Svizzera Pontificia, Colonello Elmar Mäder, on a visit to Boston as a guest of the Ancient and Honorable Artillery Company of Massachusetts (the 'AHAC'), encountered the P&Ms for the first time and invited them to visit Rome in May 2006. The Company had first encountered the Swiss Guard back in 1991 when they did a joint duty for a reception at Swiss Bank Corporation, one of the new global banks establishing themselves in the City. Later, in 2010, the Company paraded at Lancaster House for Pope Benedict XVI himself.

But the 2006 visit was the big one – the 500th anniversary of the foundation of the Pontifical Swiss Guard. After Mass at St Peter's Basilica, the P&Ms framed a body inside the barracks, where they were inspected by their three governors – the GOC London District, the Lord Mayor and the HAC Colonel Commandant. They then marched through the Bernini colonnade and up the Basilica steps into St Peter's Square, with the 'The English March' beating out on the drums and the crowds roaring their approval. Behind them came representatives of other ancient and famous regiments: the Guardia Real from Spain (white capes, black tricorn hats and halberds); des Grenadiers Fribourgeois from Fribourg (Napoleonic uniforms); the AHAC (dark-blue service dress and peaked caps); and modern Italian armed forces. Afterwards there was a reception at Castel Sant'Angelo and a re-enactment of a 1550 papal fireworks display.

During the inspection, the Colonel Commandant, General Sir Timothy Granville-Chapman, was astonished to find a member of the Company on parade wearing Second World War medals. This was Musketeer Gordon Passmore, then aged 83, who had joined the Fleet Air Arm in 1940 aged 17 and flown more than 230 missions, first on anti-submarine patrols, then on Arctic convoys and finally in the Pacific. He crashed for the first time in 1943, over the side of the escort carrier HMS *Campania*, landing upside down over a gun emplacement, dangling from his harness. His second crash came in June 1945, when he was shot down by the Japanese and spent several hours in the water, before being rescued by a British destroyer whose captain disobeyed express orders not to stop for survivors. The captain may have been influenced by the fact that Passmore was drifting towards a Japanese-occupied island where the garrison had orders to behead any captured airmen.

Bruges

Passmore's naval medals had been drawing attention from fellow matelots ever since he joined the P&Ms in 1966. Lord Mountbatten always stopped to speak to him, and Prince Philip would ask: 'Where is the naval aviator?'

Prince Philip had another reason to remember the P&Ms. In September 2006, as Colonel of the Grenadier Guards, he attended the Grenadiers' 350th anniversary in Bruges, where they had been raised back in 1656 as King Charles II's personal bodyguard in exile. Prince Philip had expressly requested the attendance of the P&Ms 'as being similarly accoutred to the original Grenadiers'.

Four hundred dignitaries, including HRH Prince Philip and the Crown Prince of Belgium, assembled in the Burg Square at Bruges, with Nijmegen Company Grenadiers, a company of Belgian grenadiers and the P&Ms, who gave a display of seventeenth-century arms drill, culminating in a musket volley fired directly in front of the VIP stand. Musketeer Jeremy Cowdry recalls looking down the barrel of his musket and seeing in the front row of the stand the two princes looking rather concerned, and Pikeman Richard Peters was close enough to hear Prince Philip say, 'You're not going to fire those bloody things at us, are you?' Fortunately, the Musketeers had been ordered to aim high and the musket fire was greeted with applause and laughter.

Prince Philip reportedly gave his equerry a rocket for not warning him in advance, but by the evening he was in high good humour, giving everyone a hard time and saying that nobody had told him we were going to fire muskets and it had frightened the life out of him!

The memory of being shot at stayed with the Prince for a long time. In February 2007, when the P&Ms paraded for the centenary of the Old Bailey, he spotted Musketeer Cowdry and went over to him, asking, 'Were you one of the shits who shot at us?'

'Yes, your Royal Highness!'

'Well done!'

At another event, when the Musketeers fired a royal salute, Prince Philip took a pace forward, looked down the line of spectators to check they were all still standing, and announced loudly: 'Missed!'

In March 2016, at a Guildhall dinner for the Commonwealth High Commissioners, Musketeer Robert Raffety felt someone fiddling with his bandoleer.

'So these are what you call your Apostles,' said Prince Philip. 'And', taking hold of Raffety's musket rest, 'this is your rest for the musket when Giving Fire?'

'Yes, Sir.'

'And you're the shits who are always trying to kill us!'

'Yes, Sir!'

Other Prince Philip one-liners include an encounter with a particularly ponderous HAC Light Cavalryman – 'You don't look very light to me!' – and a visit to the HAC Museum, where he was met by Andrew Izod, then P&M Adjutant, in lobster pot helmet and half armour – 'Are you one of the exhibits?'

Vittorio Veneto

In November 2008, the P&Ms visited Italy for the ninetieth anniversary of Vittorio Veneto, the last battle on the Italian front in the First World War. Here, the HAC 2nd Battalion had distinguished themselves by capturing the island of Papadopoli, a crucial crossing on the Piave River, which led to the collapse of the Austro-Hungarian front. The event was organised by the Italian government assisted by Alpini veterans and Michael Drewitt, an HAC veteran living in Verona who spoke fluent Italian.

The P&Ms flew (on a commercial flight at their own expense – military transport now being a thing of the past) to Venice and from there were bussed to a pre-First World War barracks in Vittorio Veneto. Here their quarters were on the third floor with no lift, with the ablutions on the other side of the parade ground. The lavatories were hole-in-the-ground affairs and, the next morning, QM Richard Ward heard terrible moans and groans coming from the lavatory area. Fearing an attack of food poisoning, he rushed over, only to find that the holes in the ground had no handles, and elderly P&Ms were having trouble getting up from the crouch position.

The first day included memorial services at military cemeteries, lunch with the Mayor of Montello and, in the evening, dinner in Conegliano, with the Alpini veterans in their green Tyrolean hats. On the second day, at the main wreath-laying ceremony, the P&Ms entered behind the

Bersaglieri, an elite Italian light infantry unit, famous for the chicken feathers they wear on their helmets and their marching speed of 180 paces per minute. The P&Ms followed at their much slower eighty paces, forming up in the town square alongside the Bersaglieri, the Carabinieri, the Italian Air Force and the Guardia di Finanza.

Then it began to rain. And it poured. The Italian president had been scheduled to arrive by helicopter but the rain was so heavy that he switched to a car, resulting in an hour's delay. When he finally appeared, he bowed briefly to the war memorial and scuttled into the town hall without even a look at his guard of honour. In the evening, the Company revived itself with a banquet at the mountaintop fortress of CastelBrando, accessible only by a funicular railway, with a P&M guard lining the near-vertical staircase to the dining hall at the top.

Vienna

In March 2011, Alderman Gavyn Arthur called Adjutant Izod to warn him that the Company would be asked to provide an escort for the funeral of Archduke Otto von Habsburg, the last Crown Prince of Austria-Hungary.

Why was this? After the Battle of Vittorio Veneto, the HAC 2nd Battalion had been stationed in Austria as part of the occupying forces. According to legend, when Emperor Charles I was exiled, the 2nd Battalion presented arms as he boarded his train. 'Look!' said the Emperor. 'My enemies salute me but my own people ignore my going!'

Crown Prince Otto, Charles I's son, was 6 years old when his family was sent into exile. When he grew up, he renounced his claim to the throne, had a long career in European politics, and died on 4 July 2011 aged 98. A P&M detachment arrived in Vienna on 7 July and found itself in the middle of a full state funeral in everything but name. Dignitaries from the old empire included the Austrian president and prime minister, the Romanian government, the Habsburg family, former monarchs King Michael of Romania and Tsar Simeon of Bulgaria, as well as the royal families of Sweden, Luxembourg and Liechtenstein.

The P&M detachment stood vigil at Crown Prince Otto's lying in state in St Stephen's Cathedral and the Requiem Mass was celebrated by seven bishops from the seven nations of the Austro-Hungarian Empire. Afterwards the P&M, alongside Habsburg family mourners, escorted the Prince's coffin to the church of the Capuchin friars, traditional resting place of the Habsburg emperors. Marching beside them was a detachment of colonels from the Austrian Defence Ministry. QM Richard Ward remembers that the colonels kept losing the step, and the Garde Regiment sergeant major kept shouting at them: *'Meine Herren! Links, rechts, links, rechts!'*

As the coffin passed through the streets, groups from villages and associations that had come from all over Austria silently joined the procession till it was more than 4 kilometres long. On arrival at the Capuchin church, a herald knocked three times on the door. From inside a Capuchin friar called out: 'Who wishes to enter?' The herald listed the Crown Prince's imperial and royal titles. The friar was not impressed by this display of worldliness and answered: 'We do not know him!' The herald knocked three times again. This time he listed Otto's academic, political and civic achievements. Again the answer was: 'We do not know him!'

A third knock.

'Who wishes to come in?'

'Otto – a mortal and a sinner.'

'Let him enter.'

Menorca

In the eighteenth century, Menorca was the Royal Navy's main station in the Mediterranean and it was here that, in 1711, the first Royal Naval hospital was established on the Isla del Rey. It survived the departure of the British in 1802 and a period of occupation by the US Navy, but eventually fell into disrepair. In 2004, a project was initiated to restore it and in 2011, on the hospital's 300th anniversary, it was opened to the public at what was billed as a joint UK–US event. The US Navy sent naval personnel and a destroyer – USS *Bulkeley*. The Royal Navy had nothing to spare, so the British ex-patriate community clubbed together to fund a small P&M detachment to represent Great Britain. The detachment was lodged on mainland Menorca and travelled to the Isla del Rey in a rubber RIB (rigid inflatable boat). The sea spray played havoc with the Pikemen's armour and on one occasion, Musketeer Charlie Deakin, leaping too enthusiastically from the quayside, bounced on the RIB's gunwale and would have landed in the sea had his comrades not grabbed him by his jerkin.

The first parade, in 100°F, was for the dedication of St George's Chapel in the hospital complex and the Royal Naval memorial. A second parade at the English Cemetery was planned as a joint US–UK event, but went awry when the Americans forgot that the British were coming (Paul Revere is turning in his grave) and started the ceremony without them. When the P&Ms arrived at the correct start time, the embarrassed Americans restarted the ceremony from the beginning, complete with a royal salute, musket fire and the national anthem played on the fife by Elder Drumbeater Roger Davenport.

Other duties

As the Army gets smaller, the P&Ms have an increasing role in maintaining their links with civilian society. In 2008, they kept the ground at St Paul's Cathedral as 'the City's Salute to the Armed Forces' and later the same summer lined the cathedral steps for the Territorial Army's 100th anniversary service, the same roles they had performed sixty years earlier in 1948 for the royal silver wedding and in 1951 at the Festival of Britain. In 2008 they took part in an historical pageant at the Royal Hospital Chelsea, in 2014 the Royal Marines' 350th anniversary and in 2016 the Royal Artillery's 300th at Larkhill, and paid return visits in 2016 with the Grenadiers to Bruges, and in 2018 to Italy for the centenary of Vittorio Veneto.

In the 2010s, the P&Ms paraded for the inauguration of two new Combined Cadet Force corps sponsored by the HAC – from the City of London Academy in Islington and the Mossbourne Community Academy in Hackney. They have also paraded twice for the Invictus Games, founded by Prince Harry to ensure that injured services personnel are not forgotten, and to inspire recovery and generate a wider understanding and respect of those who serve their country. In 2019, they took part in the launch of the British team selected for the Invictus Games 2020, and in 2024 attended the opening of a one-day summit to mark the tenth anniversary of the Games, with Prince Harry as patron.

The P&Ms

By the 1990s the Company's Second World War veterans were standing down and, for the first time in its history, most serving P&Ms had not seen active service. But a number of members are still ex-regulars who have seen active service; following the 1996 Reserve Forces Act, these have been reinforced by regimental members who have done an active service attachment. In 2024, just under 20 per cent of the Company had seen some form of active service with the British Army, ranging from Aden to Afghanistan, and one member had served in the French Foreign Legion.

When the Reserve Forces Act was introduced, defence cuts had badly damaged the regular RAMC, and reservist medics were now allowed to volunteer for active service up to the age of 65. Among them was Musketeer Colonel John Hamilton MD who, aged 60, and in the teeth of opposition from his NHS Health Trust, was accepted for temporary active service in Bosnia. After a long period of training, he embarked in 1997 on a six-month tour as a general duty MO, deployed initially in 'Slipper City' at Dalma. Here he was responsible for 1,000 troops and on call twenty-four hours a day seven days a week, dealing with everything from mine injuries to traffic accidents. Later he travelled to Banja Luka and Sanski Most, where he held clinics for refugees in bombed-out buildings with no running water, no toilets, no heating, no doors, no privacy and with all conversation via an interpreter. A year later, he did another six-month tour in Cyprus.

Another notable member, Pikeman Dominic Reid, joined the P&Ms in 2011. Dominic has acted as Pageantmaster of the Lord Mayor's Show since 1992 and as chief executive of the Invictus Games from 2014 to 2024.

Some members are distinguished by length of service. The longest serving current member is Roger Davenport, who joined in 1991 and has completed thirty-four years of service, including a tour as Elder Drumbeater. He is still a few years behind Elder Drumbeater Tubby Ayers (forty-one years on his retirement in 1966) and the record-holder, Pikeman Don Hodgson, who served in the 2nd Regiment HAC (Heavy

Anti-Aircraft) under Edward Heath in the early 1950s, joined the P&Ms in 1960 aged 30 and, when he finally returned his kit to stores in 2010, aged 80, had carried his pike for fifty years.

In the spring of 2020, the P&Ms, along with the rest of the world, were engulfed by the Covid pandemic and everything came to a halt, including the Lord Mayor's Show. During lockdown, the P&Ms discovered Zoom and WhatsApp, and stayed in touch via online chat groups and virtual wine tastings with Ye Feast, attended by the Lord Mayor and Sheriffs, held via Zoom.

In the autumn of 2020, when people began to be allowed out under rigorous social-distancing rules, the P&Ms donned white face masks to provide their first lockdown-style guard of honour for the HAC Mess Club, with everyone sitting at tables of six, set 6 feet apart from each other, a socially distanced HAC orchestra playing in the balcony at the far end of the Prince Consort Room, and guest speaker File Leader Drumbeater Simon Garrett[11] describing the damage lockdown was doing to the hospitality industry.

The final lifting of lockdown in 2022 saw the first P&M recruits course since 2019 and on it, for the first time, two female HAC veterans. Under MOD rules, women became eligible to join the HAC Regiment in 1999 and had now grown old enough to be considered for the P&Ms, one duly passing off into the Muskets and the other into the Pikes.

---

11. Commanding officer of the HAC 2004–2006 and captain of the P&Ms from September 2025.

Chapter Fourteen

The Pageant Continues

The Modern Show

There are fewer pageants now than there used to be, but the Lord Mayor's Show retains all the key features – a community embodied in physical form marching through its own streets, the blurring of boundaries between performers and spectators and, in the Lord Mayor's party, a visual acting out of the history and continuity of the show and the City it celebrates.

> Hey diddle dinkety poppety pet,
> The merchants of London they wear scarlet,
> Silk in the collar and gold in the hem,
> So merrily march the merchant men.

Ahead of the Lord Mayor's party ride the mounted band of the Household Cavalry in their full state dress, only worn when parading for royalty or the Lord Mayor. Their gold coats and black jockey caps are the oldest continually worn uniform in the British Army; designed for the restoration of King Charles II in 1660 and paid for by the Lord Mayor (Parliament had said they were too extravagant and refused to pay).

Immediately behind the band, and in front of the coach, walk four Watermen in wide-skirted scarlet coats and jockey caps, carrying oars over their shoulders and led by the Watermen's Bargemaster. These are the Doggett's Coat and Badge men, winners of the annual sculling race held on the Thames since 1715. They took over this escort duty in 1981 from the Lord Mayor's original footmen in Regency livery and bicorne hats and commemorate the days when the Lord Mayor's procession took place on the Thames.

Next comes the Lord Mayor's State Coach, though its six Shire horses are no longer provided by Whitbread's, who closed their Chiswell Street stables in 1998. The coach is now prepared for the show in a temporary glass coach house in the west entrance to Guildhall Yard, and the horses come from Waldburg Shires of Huntingdon, specialists in heavy horse hire.

The coach is uncomfortable by modern standards, rocking from side to side on a suspension system of two enormous leather straps, creating a real risk of seasickness, particularly when looking at the heaving landscape outside the coach window – Dame Fiona Woolf (Lord Mayor 2013–14), recommends locking one's gaze onto a fixed point on the horizon.

Alongside the coach, the Pikemen still march 'three and three', trying not to get trodden on by a heavy horse hoof, or squashed by a coach wheel, or get in the way of the Lord Mayor waving out of the coach window – as happened to Dame Fiona, who managed, with a particularly exuberant movement, to hook her tricorne hat on the point of an escorting pike.

Behind the coach party comes the rest of the Company with the captain at its head, in the full accoutrements of a Cromwellian cavalry officer. In 2005, the captain of the day, David Horn, an ex-Grenadier with horsey connections, borrowed Drummond, a dark bay gelding of 17 hands, from the Horse Guards and rode the whole route on horseback. Horn and Drummond got on famously, apart from an incident when

Drummond spotted two mares in front of him ridden by policewomen, and ambled up to say hello (there's life in the old dog yet ...).

The modern Show comprises some 140 floats and 7,000 participants. Many are from commercial organisations, approximately 1,800 are military personnel and a further 1,800 are children and young people. Together with 200 horses and 140 motor and steam-driven vehicles, they form a procession that is over 3 miles long and takes one hour and ten minutes to pass a spectator on the pavement.

Along the route, the skyline continues to change. Mansion House Crossing is now dominated by a vast, 278 metres high skyscraper – the unadventurously named 22 Bishopsgate, the second tallest building in Britain after The Shard, with 1 Canada Square now dropping back into third place.

Cheapside retains its 1960s' white box flavour. In New Change, the relatively tasteful Bank of England extension has been replaced by a vast, gloomy slab of smoked brown glass, presenting as a shopping mall. Things improve when the procession reaches the top of Ludgate Hill, where the harsh, 1970s' elevations of Paternoster Square have been demolished in favour of a carefully proportioned, postmodernist courtyard, encircled by classical colonnades and entered through the newly restored Temple Bar Gateway.

At the Royal Courts of Justice, while the Lord Mayor is taking his oath of loyalty, the procession falls out for lunch. In its early days, the Company picnicked in the open air of Bell Yard, a narrow passageway between the Law Courts and Chancery Lane. In 1973, with the permission of the Queen's Remembrancer, they moved inside the Law Courts to suttle in the Gothic splendour of the Bear Garden. In 2014, the venue switched to the more intimate, but still very Gothic, West Green Building. Here the P&Ms doff jerkins and armour for a hurried buffet lunch – sandwiches with the crusts cut off, sausages in buns, mini quiches, wraps and so on. But the first stop is usually a line of wine glasses emitting a soft green glow. Whisky Macs are the Army's traditional cold-weather stiffener, invented, for strictly medicinal purposes, in India around 1900 by General (Fighting Mac) MacDonald, and consisting of equal parts of green ginger wine and Scotch whisky.

Around 2 pm, the procession re-forms and returns to Mansion House by way of the Embankment. Here, in 2012, for the first time in living memory, the coach broke down. The onside rear axle seized up and, despite much heaving and pushing, proved impossible to unjam. Pageantmaster Dominic Reid gave the Lord Mayor a lift and the P&Ms returned to Mansion House as escort to the Pageantmaster's ceremonial Land Rover. Several hours later, the coach was eventually transported back to Guildhall on a recovery vehicle, where days of hammering finally freed up the eighteenth-century mechanism.

On the final stretch up Queen Victoria Street, the sky ahead of the marchers is dominated by two new skyscrapers – the Cheese Grater (Leadenhall Street, 225 metres) and the Walkie Talkie (Fenchurch Street, 160 metres).

Civic Duties

The P&Ms continue to support the Lord Mayor during his year of office. In 2003, they paraded for President Putin, the first full state visit by a Russian ruler since Tsar Alexander II in 1874 (and, given current politics, probably the last for a while). Another landmark was the 2005 state visit of Hu Jintao, General Secretary of the People's Republic of China (PRC). His visit was disrupted by crowds protesting at the PRC's treatment of political dissidents and its occupation of Tibet, and responded to by PRC-sponsored counter-demonstrations. As the P&Ms arrived at Guildhall, the two opposing demonstrations, held back by police, were creating an enormous din with gongs and whistles, but fell into relative silence as the P&Ms marched between the lines. By 2015, when Hu Jintao's successor, General Secretary Xi Jinping, visited the UK, the PRC had got its dissidents back under control, Prime Minister David Cameron was suitably fawning, and everything went much more smoothly.

The Lord Mayor still spends a significant part of his year on overseas trade visits, though recreations of the Lord Mayor's Show have mostly died out – partly due to cost, and partly the difficulty of finding suitable horses to pull the carriage. The last true carriage procession took place in June 2006, not in foreign parts but at the Royal Cornwall Show. Here, the locally recruited horses performed well, apart from a moment when they shot backwards with the coach on two wheels and the Lord Mayor clinging on for dear life, then charged forward, nearly taking out a couple of Pikemen. Musketeer John Wallace, sitting beside the commentator to explain what the P&Ms were doing, managed to distract him while this was going on, and no mention was made of it in the commentary.

In 2025, when the P&Ms escorted Lord Mayor Alistair King at the Sechseläuten parade in Zurich, the Lord Mayor solved the coach work problem by walking the entire parade route on foot.

Other Duties

The P&Ms, with their seventeenth-century uniforms and historic City connections, are a living symbol of guardianship and City ancestry. As such, they have a natural resonance with events commemorating history, community and continuity.

In 2024, P&M bookings for City institutions included the Pattenmakers, Gardeners, Bridge Ward Club, Chartered Surveyors,

Wax Chandlers, Playing Card Makers, Information Technologists, Nurses, Clothworkers, Cooks, Pewterers, Painter Stainers, Building Contractors, Builders' Merchants, World Traders, Feltmakers, Grocers, Fanmakers, Air Pilots, Investment Managers and the Guild of Freemen. Recent parades for opening ceremonies include:

2010:   the blessing of the Information Technologists' new Royal Charter at St Paul's

2010:   the presentation of the Marketors' new Charter

2010:   the presentation of the Launderers' Royal Charter in Southwark Cathedral

2011:   the opening of the Rolls Building at the Royal Courts of Justice

2023:   the opening of Temple Bar Gateway, newly relocated to Paternoster Square.

And anniversaries – an ancient tale new told:

1978:   the Tower of London's 1,000th

1989:   the Lord Mayor's 800th

2000:   Hever Castle's 1,000th

2007:   the Old Bailey's 100th

2011:   the Broderers' 450th (including the first showing of the P&Ms' embroidered new City colour)

2014:   the Tower of London marking the 100th anniversary of the start of the First World War

2015:   the Carmen's Waterloo Ball marking the 200th anniversary of Waterloo

2018:   Les Chevaliers Bretvins' 70th anniversary at Nantes in Brittany

2021: the Wax Chandlers' 650th
2024: the Pewterers' 550th.

The most important anniversary for the Company was its centenary in 2025, beginning with the blessing of the Company's three colours at St Paul's in March, then a full parade and inspection by the Lord Mayor in July, and ending in November with the P&Ms providing the mayoral guard of honour on Lord Mayor's Day 2025, a privilege traditionally performed by City and other reserve regiments.

Royal

In 2009, Adjutant Andrew Izod, struggling to book space for the P&Ms in Armoury House in fierce competition with other HAC units, wondered aloud what it would take to break the deadlock. One thing led to another, Elder Serjeant Andrew Wallis knew someone in the Lord Chamberlain's office, and when the Colonel Commandant, General Sir Timothy Granville-Chapman, wrote formally to the Palace he obtained a promise that Her Majesty would review the Company in person. At this point, as Izod recalls, 'all Armoury House facilities became magically available.'

The royal review was held in May 2010. The Company marched onto the Artillery Ground led by the Regimental Band and welcomed Prince Michael of Kent and the Company's three governors (the GOC London District, the Lord Mayor and the Colonel Commandant) with a royal salute. This was followed by the arrival of Her Majesty and the Duke of Edinburgh and a second royal salute. The Queen inspected the Company and received a loyal address from the captain and a third royal salute, this time with musket fire. As the Company marched off, the band played 'The Standard of St George' (Kenneth Alford, 1930).

Finally, the Queen and Prince Philip joined the P&Ms for a group photograph, with reporters and photographers clustering around. As Captain Paul Champness squeezed himself into his assigned place next to the Queen, one of his tassets brushed Her Majesty's thigh. Champness apologised – his armour, he said, seemed to have acquired a mind of its own. The Queen smiled and Prince Philip made a Prince Philip-like comment.[12] The press were ecstatic! 'Pikeman's Pickle!' chortled the *Daily Telegraph*; *The Sun*, more coarsely: 'Budge Up Yer Maj!' The *East Grinstead Courier* (Paul Champness's local paper) quietly proud: 'Queen Amused by East Grinstead Man'. All was taken in good part, but indicative of the extraordinary level of public attention focused on the Royal Family.

Other royal duties in the 2010s included the opening of the Rolls Building by the Queen and the service at St Paul's for her Diamond Jubilee.

Then, on the afternoon of Thursday, 8 September 2022, came the sad news of the death of Her Majesty, the proclamation of her successor scheduled for 11 am on Saturday, 10 September. The P&Ms spent the night of Friday, 9 September sleeping on the floor of Armoury House, up early next morning for breakfast alongside the HAC Band parading for the same duty, then into uniforms and armour and Captain Tony Gabb leading them in a last toast to 'Our Captain General, Her Majesty the Queen'.

Then onto the coach, accompanied for the first time in many years by a police motorcycle escort, complete with leapfrogging and whistle blowing, down to Aldermanbury. Then lining the Threadneedle Street and Cornhill approaches to the Royal Exchange. Passing between their lines, the Lord Mayor in black and gold, the Aldermen in scarlet, the

---

12. 'Keep your hands off my wife!'

State Trumpeters in gold lace and enormous jackboots, the Heralds in their brightly coloured medieval tabards, all assembling on the steps of the Royal Exchange. At 11 am, the State Trumpeters blew a fanfare and the proclamation was read out.

> Whereas it has pleased Almighty God to call to His Mercy our late Sovereign Lady Queen Elizabeth the Second of Blessed and Glorious memory … We, therefore … do now hereby with one voice and Consent of Tongue and Heart publish and proclaim that The Prince Charles Philip Arthur George is now … become our only lawful and rightful Liege Lord Charles the Third.

The national anthem played but the words had changed: 'God Save the King!'

A year later, in October 2023, King Charles III made his Coronation Year visit to the City, to thank it for its support and reconfirm its ancient rights and privileges. The new king's speech continued themes from George V's 1940 'Spirit of the City' speech, Archbishop Fisher's 1948 silver wedding speech and even Churchill's 1951 'Gog and Magog' speech.

> The United Kingdom is a 'community of communities'; an island nation in which our shared values are the force which holds us together, reminding us that there is far, far more that unites us than divides us: civility and tolerance; a sense of fairness; the British sense of humour; a sense of public service which takes us far beyond the call of duty; the instinct to co-operate, a kind of muscle-memory.

These instincts [enable] us to fulfil our duties as good citizens who understand, without having to write down or formalise them, the decencies on which our institutions and our constitution depend, as well as our relationships, one to another. [They] make us what we are and shape what we aspire to be, on these Islands that we share, cherish and … sustain.

Appendices

Appendix 1

The Spirit of the Place

The spirit of a community is visible in its customs and rituals, collective memories and images, which confirm its common identity and sense of citizenship. In ancient Rome, this communal spirit was embodied in the Lares, the domestic gods of household, family and community, an invocation of good fortune, peace and prosperity.

The City is particularly rich in institutions and images that pick up on these archetypal patterns. The P&Ms follow in a long line of guardians who watch over the City, from the giants Gog and Magog in Guildhall to the dragon at the entrance to Fleet Street. Their role is strictly symbolic. The peace and harmony of the City is such that the Lord Mayor does not need a real bodyguard – a message that the 1956 Soviet delegation struggled to understand, and was made explicit by Lord Mayor Sir Allan Davis at Heathrow Airport in 1986.

And there is the armour, a natural symbol of strength and permanence. Again the Pikemen are relative newcomers to this City tradition of the 'arm'd man'.

In one version of the Gog Magog legend, Magog appears as a Roman knight wearing armour and carrying sword and shield, representing civilisation and order, in combat with the wild man Gog personifying the forces of chaos.[13]

---

13. Both now preside together in Guildhall as joint protectors of the City.

From at least the early eighteenth century the Lord Mayor's bodyguard included an 'ancient knight', visible in Hogarth's 1747 engraving of the Lord Mayor's Show at the back of the mayoral party, and later described as the Lord Mayor's Champion. By the nineteenth century, this had become a full escort of mounted knights wearing tilting armour borrowed from the Tower of London. Alongside them rode an even more eccentric bodyguard, known as the 'man in brass', wearing a suit of bronze armour designed and cast for him by the brass founders and braziers.

During the nineteenth century, the Lord Mayor's coach was also escorted by a troop of lancers or hussars. In the 1930s, when the cavalry regiments were mechanised, this mounted escort role was taken over by the Horse Guards who, in the tradition of the arm'd man, wear steel helmets and cuirasses, originally taken from the French cuirassiers they defeated at Waterloo. As with the Household Cavalry band, their presence is said to be an acknowledgement of the City's financing of the band's original gold state uniforms.

Appendix 2

Boundaries

The guardians of the place are the guardians of its boundaries, and the physical presence of the P&Ms on duty is a symbolic beating of the bounds.

On Lord Mayor's Day, the Lord Mayor travels to the western edge of his territory at the junction of Fleet Street and the Strand, where he enters the Royal Courts of Justice to swear allegiance to the Crown.

This border, between the City and Crown territory, was originally marked by the baroque Temple Bar gateway, built in 1672 by Sir Christopher Wren. In 1878, the gateway was dismantled as part of a road-widening scheme and moved to Theobalds Park in Hertfordshire. The City's western entrance is now guarded by the Temple Bar Memorial; a granite column topped with a dragon (from the City's coat of arms) looking down the Strand towards Whitehall. In the early years of her reign, when visiting the City, the Queen's coach would stop here and the Lord Mayor would offer her the City's sword, which she would accept and then return, in a visual demonstration of her confidence in his government.

In 2004, the Temple Bar gateway was returned to the City to serve as the entrance to the new Paternoster Square. In March 2023, it was officially reopened by HRH the Duke of Gloucester representing the King. The P&Ms paraded on the south or City side of the gates, while on the north side, the Duke's herald knocked three times for admittance. There was a drumroll, two Musketeers pulled the gates open, and trumpeters played 'The Pageantmaster's Fanfare'. The Lord Mayor presented the Duke of Gloucester with the City's sword, which the Duke duly returned and the Bread Street Choir sang Mendelssohn's setting of Psalm 121:

> Lift thine eyes, O lift thine eyes to the mountains, whence cometh help.

To the east, the City is bounded by the Tower of London, built by William the Conqueror to keep unruly Londoners under control. The boundary between the City and the Tower Liberty was in dispute for many years, particularly after James I transferred a slice of the City's eastern territory to the Tower. The resulting tension was still apparent in 1741 when the mid-year appointment of a new Lord Mayor (the previous one had died in office) involved him taking his oath of loyalty at the Tower. The Tower governor, Brigadier Adam Williamson, was determined that the City should not use the occasion to assert any rights over his territory. He demanded that the Lord Mayor should enter the Tower Liberty as a private citizen and that the military escort should be provided solely by his own troops. To his chagrin, he found that the Lord Mayor was entitled to be escorted by the HAC as his personal bodyguard who, complained Williamson, 'it seems always march before the Lord Mayor even to the bar in Westminster hall'.

Williamson still meant to conduct the visit on his own terms and, as soon as the Lord Mayor's coach entered the Tower Liberty, he surrounded it with Yeomen Warders, marching 'two and two' on either side 'to keep up our right to the ground he marched over'. The HAC bodyguard was met by Williamson's Tower Hamlets Militia, lined up and facing off against them. The oath-taking itself was conducted with reasonable civility, though Williamson thought the Lord Mayor's party was not sufficiently deferential, and declined the usual invitation to dine afterwards at Guildhall, pleading a bad cold.

Since then, relations with the Tower have improved. The HAC provided the Tower's military garrison in the First World War, and on their departure presented the Yeomen Warders with the lantern that they still use each night in the Ceremony of the Keys. Since 1947, the HAC, now represented by the P&Ms, have also played an annual bowls match against the Warders in the Tower Moat, which by tradition the P&Ms always lose.

The City–Tower rivalry was re-enacted at the Tower of London's 1,000th anniversary in May 1976, when the P&Ms escorted the Lord Mayor and his party in two landaus from Mansion House to Tower Hill. After a brief ceremony at All Hallows-by-the-Tower, in an image of the HAC's 1741 visit, they took up positions along the City boundary, facing off against an opposing line of Yeomen Warders.

Appendix 3

Americans

The bonding value of a shared meal was demonstrated in 1943, when American and British military staff, meeting to plan the invasion of Normandy, found that their different methods and cultures were generating friction and distrust. To help bridge the gap a series of regular dinners were planned, the first taking place under the aegis of General Eisenhower and Lord Nuffield, and leading to a noticeable improvement in Anglo-American military relations.

This was the origin of the British-American Forces Dining Club, which continues to this day. Most meetings are now held at Armoury House, with the P&Ms providing the ceremonial guard of honour (Americans would say the honor guard), though in 1997 the dinner was held in the Great Hall of Lincoln's Inn, and in 1998 at the Tower of London with Prince Philip in attendance.

The year 1943 also saw the appearance of the shorter-lived 'Chicago Club' – an association of 300 servicemen from Chicago which, in December 1943, arranged a ceremonial exchange of colours with the City at Mansion House. The Pikes escorted the Lord Mayor and presented the Union Jack and City colour to the Chicagoans, receiving in return Old Glory and the City of Chicago colours.

In 1984, the Company was invited to Baltimore to take part in the 350th anniversary of the foundation of the State of Maryland and to honour its British heritage. In 1996, they attended a return visit to England by the governor of Maryland, to present Her Majesty the Queen with 'two arrows of the land', the rent originally due to the Crown, and dedicate a plaque at the grave of Lord Baltimore at St Giles-in-the-Fields in Camden.

But the HAC's longest American connection is with the Ancient and Honourable Artillery Company of Massachusetts (the 'AHAC' or the 'Ancients'). Founded in 1638 by HAC member Robert Keayne as a daughter regiment of the HAC, its members include eleven Medal of Honor recipients and four US presidents, one of whom, John Kennedy, delivered his presidential acceptance speech from the AHAC's headquarters at Faneuil Hall. On his assassination in 1963, the P&Ms sent the Ancients a telegram expressing their deepest regret and commiserations.

The modern connection between the AHAC and the HAC began in 1887, when a party of Ancients visited England for Queen Victoria's Golden Jubilee and were received by the HAC as honoured guests. Since then, the two organisations have made reciprocal visits roughly once every decade. The P&Ms first became involved in the 1950s when they began to provide ceremonial guards for the Ancients' Fall Field Tours to Britain, but it was not until 1988 that the Company visited Boston itself as part of the HAC delegation for the AHAC's 350th June Day parade on Boston Common. The P&Ms have featured in every Boston visit since and in 2014, when the MOD declined to support the participation of the HAC Regiment, they stepped up to become the main HAC marching detachment.

In the summer of 2020, the P&Ms were booked to appear at the opening ceremony of Plymouth 400 to mark the founding of Plymouth Massachusetts in 1620. Alas, this was disrupted by the Covid pandemic and subsequent lockdown, and the celebrations were cancelled.

Appendix 4

Roast Beef

When mighty Roast Beef was the Englishman's food,
It ennobled our veins and enriched our blood.
Our soldiers were brave and our courtiers were good
Oh! the Roast Beef of old England,
And hey! For old English Roast Beef!
From 'The Roast Beef of Old England',
lyrics by Henry Fielding, 1731

This ancient tune was played for many years at the beginning of formal dinners, though nowadays the march from Handel's 1725 opera *Scipione* (the Grenadiers' slow march) is more usual.

The social significance of a shared meal may be enhanced by formal dress, ceremony, toasts and speeches. A particularly ebullient touch is the formal presentation of the main dish, the Baron of Beef, symbolising the Spirit of Plenty.

The P&Ms provided their first escort to the Baron of Beef at the HAC St George's Day dinner in 1925, where the beef's entry, carried by a cook escorted by a drumbeater and four Pikemen, was greeted with prolonged cheers and, on being set down, was saluted by the Pikemen as an honoured guest.

> No foreign mess shall ere prevail
> O'er soup made from the ox's tail
> Which with that monarch among fish
> The mighty turbot on his dish
> Heralds the coming of the chief
> Of British foods – the Roast of Beef
> And, when the beef has played its part
> The never-failing apple tart
> Prepares the trenchermen to pick
> At cheese and crashing celery stick
> And praise the founders of the gorge
> The noble Guild of Uncle George.
>
> Anon, *HAC Journal*, 1925

In 1932, the Royal Society of St George invited the P&Ms, as lineal descendants of the 1537 Fraternity of St George, to provide a guard of honour for the St George's Day meetings of its City branch at the Abercorn Rooms in the Great Eastern Hotel, Liverpool Street. This continued for many years, with a second guard being added for national meetings of the Society at the Savoy.

At the 1935 meeting of the Royal Society, the P&M escort was led by two Pioneers followed by a drumbeater, Pikemen and Musketeers and the ensign, then the beef carried shoulder-high by four large chefs, and then another six Pikemen. As the procession reached the centre of the top table, the ensign and the cooks fell out facing the president to lay the beef on the table, before resuming the procession and passing out of the hall.

Second World War rationing put an end to meat-based celebrations for more than a decade, and the reappearance of the Baron of Beef in April 1952 at the Royal Society's annual dinner, escorted once again by the P&Ms, was a hugely significant event.

It was followed in November 1953 by the reappearance of the Baron of Beef at the Lord Mayor's Banquet. The *Yorkshire Post* and *Glasgow Herald* were particularly heartened by this sign of returning prosperity:

> 800 guests, the illuminated figures of the newly restored Gog and Magog, music by the Royal Artillery Orchestra. Menu: clear turtle soup (Sherry and Punch); river trout Meunière (1949 vintage Rhine wine); Baron of beef, jacket potatoes and French salad (1945 champagne); roast partridge, game chips and braised celery (claret cup); strawberry soufflé of St George.

Roast beef continues as the central feature of St George's Day dinners. In 1996, during the height of the mad cow disease panic, the EU imposed a ban on British beef exports and a month later in April 1996, the HAC St George's Day dinner tentatively offered a non-beef option. No one (including guest of honour Princess Anne) took it.

And there is the much older tradition of the boar's head:

> The boar's head in hand bear I,
> Bedeck'd with bay and rosemary.
> And I pray you, my masters, be merry
> *Quot estis in convivio*[14]
>
> The boar's head, as I understand,
> Is the rarest dish in all this land,
> Which thus bedeck'd with a gay garland
> Let us *servire cantico*.[15]
>
> Anon, fifteenth-century carol

---

14. 'As many as are at the feast'.
15. 'Let us serve with a song.'

The Boar's Head Ceremony precedes that of the Baron of Beef by several centuries. It is particularly associated with Christmas festivities, and is still celebrated at Queen's College, Oxford and in the City by the Butchers' and Armourers' companies. The P&Ms have on several occasions been privileged to escort the boar's head into Armourers' Hall to the beat of the drum, while a choir from the Guildhall School of Music sings the 'Boar's Head Carol'.

Appendix 5

St Mary-le-Bow

St Mary-le-Bow is the City's second church after St Paul's and, to be a true Londoner, one must be born within the sound of its bells.

Badly damaged in the war, its restoration and reconsecration took place in 1964. 'A great day to be a Londoner' shouted the headline in the *Evening Standard*. The Lord Mayor, his guest of honour Queen Elizabeth the Queen Mother, and a pearly king and queen representing the spirit of the Londoner, entered through the church's north door and passed between two lines of Pikemen.

Meanwhile, outside the church, the Bishop of London approached the west door, where he knocked three times with his crook and invoked the divine presence:

> Open me the gates of righteousness, that I may go into them
> and give thanks. Lift up your heads, O ye gates, and be ye lift
> up ye everlasting doors; and the King of Glory shall come in.

The rector threw open the door, the P&Ms stood aside, and the Bishop was presented with the keys to the church. Later, during the consecration, he took full possession of the ground in the name of Christ, tracing the signs of The Cross and of Alpha and Omega with his staff on the floor, and proclaiming:

Enter O Lord this house we beseech thee and within the hearts of thy faithful people establish for thyself an everlasting habitation, that this church which is rebuilt to thy glory may be gloried also by thine abiding presence.

Appendix 6

The East India Club

Another unusual P&M duty is to guard the Lord Mayor at his annual luncheon at the East India Club. The event goes back to 1918, when the Lord Mayor of the day dined as a guest of the Eccentric Club, its membership drawn from the theatre, music hall, and descendants of the notorious Pelican Club, as patronised by Galahad Threepwood in P.G. Wodehouse's Blandings novels.

The Lord Mayor's visit to the Eccentric Club became a regular fixture in his calendar and in 1985, when the club was closed for renovation, the event was moved, temporarily it was thought, to the East India Club in St James's Square. A year later, the Eccentric Club closed its doors permanently and the largest body of its members transferred to the East India, bringing with them the Eccentric Clock (whose hands move anti-clockwise instead of clockwise) and the tradition of the Lord Mayor's visit.

In 2018, the centenary of the original event was commemorated by a special luncheon attended by the incumbent Lord Mayor and seven former Lord Mayors. It was on this occasion that the P&Ms were first asked to provide a guard of honour, a duty that continues and is the Lord Mayor's only regular engagement outside the City.

Appendix 7

Oak Apple Day

The ancient festival of Oak Apple Day on 29 May marks the anniversary of King Charles II's restoration in 1660. The oak apple theme refers to his escape after the Battle of Worcester, when he hid in an oak tree from the pursuing Roundheads.

Northampton has its own particular reason for celebrating Oak Apple Day. In 1675, fifteen years after the restoration, the largely wood-built town was devastated by a great fire. King Charles came to their assistance by providing over 1,000 tons of timber to help the rebuilding and halving the town's taxes for seven years. As a mark of gratitude, Northampton erected a statue of the King on the roof of All Saints' Church, Northampton, which, every Oak Apple Day, the Mayor of Northampton crowns with a wreath of oak leaves hoisted on a long pole – a distinctly tricky exercise.

By invitation of the Lord Lieutenant of Northamptonshire, the P&Ms have for some years now provided a guard of honour at this ancient ceremony, the Musketeers wearing sprigs of oak leaves in their hats and, as the Mayor crowns the statue, firing a musket volley.

Appendix 8

Drill and Display

A recent P&M recruit who had served in Afghanistan was heard to say that he would rather be shot at by the Taliban than do drill. But for the original P&Ms, good drill was not just a matter of discipline, but essential to battlefield survival.

In 1643, on their march to relieve Gloucester, the HAC-officered City brigade stopped Prince Rupert's cavalry from outflanking them by deploying from a marching column into an extended line, 1,000 abreast and 6 deep – a particularly difficult manoeuvre to perform on the move. An astonished Rupert withdrew, swearing he thought all the Roundheads in England were there.

A month later at the Battle of Newbury,[16] the HAC-officered Red Trained Band, under heavy royalist artillery fire for several hours, suffered costly casualties and finally broke formation to seek shelter under a tumulus. Prince Rupert immediately ordered a cavalry charge, which should have swept them away along with the whole of the Parliament southern flank. Instead, their HAC officers pulled them back into combat formation within a few seconds, just in time to meet Rupert's charge with a solid hedge of pikes and volley musket fire.

When Goold Walker re-formed the P&Ms 300 years later, his main reference book was *Direction for Musters*, printed by Thomas Buck and Roger Daniel in Lombard Street in 1638, and his focus was personal

---

16. This is based on Jon Day's interpretation of the battle in *Gloucester & Newbury 1643: The Turning Point of the Civil War* (2007).

drill, with early displays consisting of the postures of the pike and marching up and down a bit. This was impressive enough in 1925 and the Company's slow speed of eighty paces per minute (designed for seventeenth-century marching in heavy kit over rough ground) was particularly remarked on. A journalist wrote:

> 'Drill' would be too inadequate a term to apply to their slow, rhythmic movements and such commands, spoken without haste, as 'Order your pikes', 'Port your pikes' and 'Charge for horse and draw your swords!' had the sound of romance about them.

Musketeers appeared for the first time in 1930 at the HAC Regimental Sports Day, going through the thirty-four postures of the musket, ending with: 'Give fire breast high!' (i.e. 'Don't fire high – aim at the middle of the body').

At the 1935 Tower Pageant, GW introduced an ambitious series of musket and pike movements based on Barriffe, with the Pikes as the central formation and the Muskets forming and re-forming geometrically around them – reminiscent to a 1930s' audience of the formation dance displays in a Hollywood Busby Berkeley musical.

In 1936, on the march from Huntingdon, two detachments of Musketeers marched in front of and behind the central pike block in a recognisable Barriffe formation. On arrival at Hinchingbrooke, the display reverted to the old 'postures' formula. A Pikeman complained that their perfect display of the postures of the pike was greeted with a distinct lack of applause, while the Musketeers 'loaded in thirty-four desperately slow movements, pooped off one round, and got a big hand from the home folks'.

The 1950 Royal Tournament saw the first full display of the Company deploying to meet a notional cavalry attack, with a mass of fifty

Pikemen drawing swords and charging for horse, and a thin edge of ten Musketeers deploying and firing on the flanks, a five-to-one ratio which reflected the extreme shortage of muskets at this time. During the Civil War, the preferred ratio would have been two pikemen to three musketeers.

The deficiency in muskets continued throughout the 1950s, with most guards consisting solely of Pikes, and Musketeers parading as Pikemen. The Musket Division was not fully built up again until the early 1960s, when the Company could again provide full displays of the formations and tactics described by Barriffe.

Nowadays (following Barriffe), the Company's order of march is a solid central block of thirty to forty Pikemen, the colour guard marching in the middle, a musket division marching in front and another covering the rear. On halting, the whole formation does a quarter turn to form a battle line, with the pike block now in the centre and a musket division covering each flank. From here, the Musketeers can be deployed into suitable firing positions (single or double line, volley fire, forlorn files etc.). In the event of a cavalry attack, the Pikemen charge (i.e. level) their pikes, the Muskets fire a volley and then, as the enemy cavalry attack, fall back under cover of the pike hedge.

In most of these displays the enemy is imaginary. But at the 1935 Tower Pageant the P&Ms were attacked by 'real' Saracens, charging on foot and waving scimitars. In 2008 at the Chelsea Royal Hospital Pageant, in a recreation of the Glorious Revolution of 1688, the P&Ms played the army of William of Orange, chasing off the forces of King James II, represented by a detachment of Household Cavalry, some of whose horses reacted to the pike hedge and musket fire by trying to leave the arena backwards. Two years later at the British Military Tournament, the P&Ms faced down another cavalry charge, this time by Prince Rupert's royalists, again driven off by musket fire.

Appendix 9

The Weather

The Pikes first learned the corrosive effect of rain on armour at the 1926 Lord Mayor's Show. At Huntingdon ten years later, this institutional memory seems to have been lost, the P&M scribe noting with astonishment that they discovered 'all too speedily that seventeenth-century equipment was not made for anything but stately motion and marching ... the pikes got steadily rustier and the plumes more wispy.'

Later that year, at the Lord Mayor's Show, the problem was wind. The Pike Division was a forest of flags, borrowed from the Tower Pageant and echoing the British Legion processions of the time. At the Mansion House crossing, the flag bearers were hit by a 60-mile-an-hour gale and the crowds were much entertained by their attempts to keep their banners under control. Half a mile further on, at the corner of New Bridge Street, the banner bearers were buffeted again by cold blasts of wind coming up from the river. On the way back along Queen Victoria Street, a Pikeman's helmet blew off and went bowling along on its rim.

When the Pikes took on the mayoral bodyguard role in 1946, their first three shows were dry, but in 1949 it poured and poured.

> The Show is held you will remember
> What'er the weather in November ...
> The date, perhaps is not the best

> For gentlemen so richly dressed
> Whose raiment gay just won't stay dry
> When Juno weeps from clouds on high
> No chance to dry their soak'd attire
> Except before the long room fire.

The Household Cavalry donned long purple capes, spreading majestically over their horses' flanks, and the Lord Mayor's coachman and footmen put on long white impermeables. But the embarrassed Pikemen had nothing suitable and ended up wearing khaki gas capes. Afterwards, they hurriedly commissioned a theatrical designer to produce twelve Jacobean-style waterproof overcoats.

> The Company's finance committee
> Willing to show a grain of pity
> One thirty pounds did authorise
> Twelve capes to buy of varied size
> Now Pikeman clad in capes of fawn
> Get dry to bed before the dawn.

These Jacobean overcoats were used in the wet Novembers of the 1950s. In the 1960s, the weather improved and the overcoats were forgotten. Andrew Izod, who joined in 1974, remembers '12 huge fawn cloaks with hoods like massive duffel coats hung from the rafters of the P&M changing room. They were never spoken of, let alone worn, and I did hear later that they were considered totally impractical for pike drill.'

Another long wet weather spell began in November 2008 when the P&Ms visited Vittoria Veneto. The parade stood for a long time, in the town square in heavy rain, waiting for the president of Italy to arrive. Fortunately, the P&Ms were wearing capes borrowed by QM

Richard Ward from the Grenadier Guards, which kept off the worst of the weather. Then Ward noticed the Musketeers swaying back and forth. 'Oh dear,' he thought, 'somebody is going to faint, but then I realised – the brims of their hats were filling with water and, getting bored, they were trying to empty the contents onto their neighbours.'

Back in the UK, Ward returned the borrowed capes to the Grenadiers and found sixty replacements in an army surplus store in Leeds. The Guards Museum tailor sewed on Venetian red collars and they were used on a succession of wet Lord Mayor's Shows from 2012 to 2017. At the 2018 show, the day looked dry enough to leave the capes behind, and it was only at the very end, as the P&Ms arrived at the gates of Armoury House, that it began to rain. Unfortunately, they were now scheduled to take part in the post-Lord Mayor's Show photograph alongside the active regiment, whose uniforms were a good deal more waterproof than those of the P&Ms. The elaborate photoshoot lasted for an hour while the rain got heavier and heavier. By the end, the Pikemen, like the Tin Man in *The Wizard of Oz*, had rusted almost completely solid.

Hot weather is more manageable, but still a challenge. When the Pikes paraded in Arizona in 1970, the temperature was 108°F and the dye from their tunics turned their underwear red in the heat. In 2006, on a hot summer's duty at Buckingham Palace, Prince Philip likened the Pikes to a line of pressure cookers. He asked Pikeman Richard Jackson, 'Are you hot in that armour?'

'Yes Sir, very.'

He touched Jackson's breastplate. 'That *is* hot! Can you fry eggs on it?'

'Of course, Sir. How would you like them done?'

'Sunny side up, please!'

Appendix 10

Organisation, Uniforms and Equipment

Hierarchy

The Company is modelled on a seventeenth-century foot company. In command is the captain with his second in command, the lieutenant, and an HQ unit comprising the adjutant, the adjutant's clerk, the QM (quartermaster), Elder Serjeant (the sergeant major), treasurer, Master Sutler and Harbinger Serjeant.

Underneath this, the main body is divided into two principal divisions of Pikemen and Musketeers, each commanded by a divisional ensign and serjeant. Each division is further divided into files commanded by a file leader. Ye Musik is a separate division commanded by the Elder Drumbeater and made up of drumbeaters and fifers, expanded for important occasions with musicians borrowed from the HAC Band and Corps of Drums, the Foot Guards and even the occasional, musically inclined Yeomen Warder.

The Captain

The first captain, Colonel Farrington, held the position from 1925 until his death in 1941. Nowadays the appointment is for a three-year tour of duty, usually beginning in November to coincide with the start of the civic year. The captain's armour is the same armour as originally worn by Colonel Farrington, and his sword, a gift to the Company, is engraved on the blade: 'Colonel Frank Farrington, Captain, Company of Pikemen 1925'.

As his badge of office, the captain carries a leading staff, a 4-foot high shaft topped by a metal finial. The present shaft was made from a length of American hickory presented by the AHAC in 1995. The finial (a Pikeman surrounded by a design of 'S's and reversed 'S's) was made by West Dean College and is copied from the head of a leading staff held in the Royal Armouries.

Uniforms and Accoutrements

Uniforms

The P&M uniforms, comprising jacket and breeches worn over stockings with knee ties, are made from napped wool, an even, solid material that is warm in winter, breathes naturally in summer and is relatively waterproof in anything but the heaviest downpour. Their colour is Venetian red (sometimes called brick red), a few shades darker than Guards scarlet. The Puritan-style white collar and cuffs, referred to as 'Ye Linen', require a continuous cycle of washing, boiling, starching and ironing. The collar ties are fastened at the throat with three separate knots said to represent the three persons of the Holy Trinity.

Ye Musik's uniforms also feature simple slashed sleeves and leggings with gold lace and buttons along the length of the slash. Officer uniforms are similar but with the gold lace and buttons on their sleeves and leggings set across the slash at five equally spaced intervals.

Rank is denoted by the width of lace worn on the linen collars and cuffs, the positioning of the sash and the complexity of the uniform itself. Lastly, officers wear thigh-length riding boots and spurs and all others wear shoes tied with cloth bows.

Pikemen

The Pikemen wear harnesses of armour consisting of backplate, and breastplate with infantry tassets (non-articulated). Their original armour is said to have been made by car panel beaters, accounting perhaps for its smooth, somewhat art deco style. It has been replaced several times since 1925 but remains essentially the same.

Headwear is a morion or pot hat. The first morions resembled a steel jockey cap, but were soon replaced by a more authentic design with a domed crown and downwards-sloping wide brim, reminiscent of a firefighter's helmet. The current design, considered more authentic yet, has a higher crown and narrower brim.

The pikes are 12 feet long with a tassel at the bottom of the blade, allegedly designed to stop blood running down the shaft and making the pikeman's hands slip. Although shorter than their seventeenth-century originals, they are still difficult to handle, and there is always a risk of stabbing the ceiling or getting into a fight with a chandelier. A stock of half pikes is kept for low ceiling duties, some of which are said to be nineteenth-century naval boarding pikes. In the 1990s, QM David Horn constructed several 'dismountable' pikes based on the joints used by chimney sweeps for their sweeping brushes. This formed the basis for the modern generation of dismountable pikes made up of two 6-foot sections, screwed together for high ceiling duties, but also available for use, using only the top half, for low ceiling duties.

The Company's other pole arms are partisans carried by officers, halberds carried by serjeants, and spontoons carried by file leaders escorting the Company's colours.

Muskets

The Musketeers wear large-brimmed, black felt hats adorned with an extravagant red ostrich feather on the rear brim and carry matchlock muskets and rests. They wear leather jerkins over the basic uniform and a bandolier adorned with twelve 'apostles', a pouch and a powder flask.

Originally, the apostles contained a measured charge, the pouch held lead balls and cloth patches for tamping down the 'round', and the powder flask a quantity of fine quality powder to fill the priming pan. A slow-burning match cord was attached to the swan neck on the breech mechanism, which, when the trigger was pulled, snapped down into the priming pan (flash-in-the-pan) and fired the musket.

The first Musketeers also wore a sword and steel morion exactly like the Musketeer supporter on the HAC coat of arms. However, these caused difficulties with the musket drills – the sword was abandoned and the morion replaced with the present cavalier-style hat.

The original 1930 muskets and their replacements through to the 1980s were working black powder matchlocks, which required anything up to thirty-four individual movements to load and fire. This did not sit well with the livelier displays of the post-war period and they were replaced by new muskets with a much simpler firing mechanism based on a Martini-Henry action dating from the 1870s (as featured in the film *Zulu*). Non-functional versions of the apostles, pouch and powder flask were retained for visual accuracy.

Around 2000, a contract for twenty-two replica muskets was placed with the Royal Armouries in Leeds. By then, Martini-Henry actions were scarce, and the new muskets (still in service) incorporated Greener actions, which were similar but more readily available. They are smooth bore with proofed barrels, and categorised and licensed as shotguns. They are also remarkably heavy, weighing over 11lb. This new generation of muskets cost £1,850 each – far too much for the P&Ms to fund on their own. An appeal was set up and each musket is named after the sponsor who paid for it. These names include: Goldsmith, Carpenter, Grocer, Furniture Maker, Chartered Accountant, Haberdasher, Cutler,

Ferroner (the Ironmongers), Clothworker, Draper and Armourer. Recently, three more muskets using the same Greener action have been built from scratch by Musketeer armourer Jon Baker, who has also deactivated most of the original black power muskets so that they can be taken abroad[17] on non-firing duties.

Pioneers

The Company included from its early years two Pioneers, marching at the head of the column carrying a morning star mounted on a flail, which, in theory, they would swing to clear the way. This was discontinued in the early 2000s, not so much on health and safety grounds (the spiked balls were made from rubber set with sponge spikes) but because it was decided that they were not period authentic.

Money

Members who pass the recruits' course are provided with their arms and accoutrements by the Company, but serve without pay and fund their own travel expenses.

The Company's ceremonial role requires a high standard of turnout and basic kit is regularly replaced, the cost covered by the Company's somewhat erratic income from its appearances at private events and the subscriptions of its members.

A full re-equipment is carried out every twenty years or so and requires a major fundraising exercise. The most recent re-equipment project in 2024 cost around £300,000.

---

17. Customs have become increasingly suspicious of any form of weapon, irrespective of its function or the organisation transporting it.

Appendix 11

Ye Musik Division

Drums and drumbeaters were an essential part of a seventeenth-century army. Most soldiers could not read or write and had no means of knowing the time and their lives were regulated by drumbeats. On the battlefield tactical orders would be sent from the commander's drummer and relayed by regimental and company drummers through the army. Drumbeats were probably also used to set the marching pace.

The P&M's Musik Division dates from the first days of the Company. A drumbeater (Tubby Ayers) complete with drum appeared in the original 1925 line-up, which soon expanded to two and later four drums, with fifers added in the 1990s. Drumbeaters are attired in a similar fashion to Musketeers, but with lighter-coloured jerkins and grey felt hats, and are commanded by the Elder Drumbeater.

The Drums

The Company's first drums were 21 inches in height and 14 inches in diameter, making them rather long and thin. They tended to bounce on the hip and even an experienced drummer like Tubby Ayers missed the drumhead occasionally, much to the amusement of his comrades. These drums were actually quite inaccurate for the mid-seventeenth century and when Jonathan Horne became Elder Drumbeater in the late

1980s, he immediately set about researching the correct specification.[18] Few drums survive from the period but he obtained access to a drum in the Royal Armouries and Drake's Drum at Buckland Abbey in Devon. There was also Rembrandt's famous painting *The Night Watch* in the Rijksmuseum. These all indicated that drums of the period were quite large – around 22½ inches high by 20 inches in diameter. A new set of four drums was commissioned and delivered in 1990. These initially had pigskin heads but were found to be unplayable when wet and were replaced with American-made plastic heads, which were indistinguishable from real skin. These drums remained in use until 2018, when a new set of four were purchased as part of the re-equipment programme. They were blessed by the Company's chaplain, The Reverend David Reindorp, in a ceremony at Chelsea Old Church. The Company therefore possesses eight drums, all of which are useable, but it is unusual for more than four to be in use at the same time.

The Fifes

In 1973, the Company borrowed two flute-players from the HAC Corps of Drums for the Berlin Tattoo and intermittently thereafter, including the 1978 Beating of the Bounds at the Tower of London and the Royal Artillery Beating Retreat on Horse Guards in 1986.

Beginning in the late 1980s, Elder Drumbeater Jonathan Horne began actively to expand the Musik Division. Many of the new members

---

18. He was well qualified to do so – a recognised authority on antiques, he published a series of high-quality reference books, was chair of the British Antique Dealers' Association in 2001–2004, and in 2005, with Lord Brooke, a former arts minster, founded the Guild of Arts Scholars (since 2014 the Worshipful Company of Art Scholars).

were ex-HAC Corps of Drums who could play drum or flute and the standard of music improved hugely. Some fifes were acquired from the US, and Drumbeaters Roger Davenport and Peter Grove taught themselves to play.

A fife is a basic flute with just one blowhole and six finger holes. There is evidence that fifes were used in seventeenth-century armies, though, from pictorial evidence, they appear to have been longer than those used by the Company, which are based on those used by the British Army in the mid-eighteenth century, and are still used by fife and drum bands in New England, where traditions inherited from the British Army survive.[19]

The Music

Before 1991, the Company had occasionally marched to music provided, where available, by a military band. Pre-war favourites, played at the Tower and Huntingdon pageants, included 'We be Soldiers Three', 'Lillibulero', 'Soldier, Soldier, Won't You Marry Me?' and 'Dashing Away with the Smoothing Iron'. When the Company appeared at the Royal Tournament in 1950, the programme described its slow march as 'We be Soldiers Three' and its quick march as 'Dashing Away with the Smoothing Iron' – the latter as a reference to the time spent by members laundering and starching their snowy white collars and cuffs. These had been forgotten by the time Ye Musik became so-named in the 1990s. At this point, fifes were introduced and a source of suitable seventeenth-century tunes found in Playford's *The Dancing Master*,

---

19. When the Army was modernised following the Crimean War, the fife was given five keys, which is the instrument still used by the Army's Corps of Drums and allows a much greater range of music to be played.

first published in 1651 and containing popular dance tunes of the day, many of which are also suitable for marching.

The Company's repertoire is mainly, but not exclusively, based on tunes of the sixteenth and seventeenth centuries, many taken from Playford with 'Gathering Peascods' and 'Sellenger's Round' being particular favourites. During inspections and other static events, Ye Musik plays more ambitious compositions, including Henry VIII's 'Pastime with Good Company' and a selection of English airs. More modern marching tunes have also been added, including 'Do You Hear the People Sing?' from *Les Misérables* and a First World War medley.

When the Company charges pikes as a general salute, the Musik plays the traditional 'Scipio' march but at the end of the Lord Mayor's Show, when the new Lord Mayor appears on the balcony of Mansion House to receive the Company's salute, a new tradition has been introduced when the fifes play a short piece associated with the Lord Mayor's name or known background, career or hobbies. Thus, in 2010 for Lord Mayor Michael Bear, the fifes played 'The Teddy Bears' Picnic' and in 2013 for Lord Mayor Fiona Woolf, 'Who's Afraid of the Big Bad Wolf?'.

Appendix 12

The Colours

In the seventeenth century, every company in a regiment had its own colour, carried as a rallying point for its members.

In 1925, the Company, referencing the HAC's origins in the 1537 Guild of St George and the St Gorge's Cross on the HAC coat of arms, adopted as its standard 'Argent a cross gules'. This was confirmed in the Company's Royal Warrant granted in 1955 and, in 1987, this colour was formally presented to the Company by Her Majesty The Queen.

In 2002, the Company obtained permission from Her Majesty's Inspector of Colours to carry a second, sovereign's colour bearing the same royal cypher (the ER initials of the sovereign reversed and interlaced) as the Grenadier Guards. The sovereign's colour was paraded for Her Majesty at the royal review of 2010 and is carried on state occasions and when a member of the Royal Family is present.

In 2024, on the death of the Queen, the P&Ms applied to the College of Arms for permission to replace the Queen's cypher with that of the new king – CR reversed and interlaced. The College, however, could find no record of any earlier approval to carry the royal cypher. The Company responded by producing a photograph of the 2010 royal review, in which Her Majesty can be seen sitting under the colour displaying her royal cypher. The College of Arms conceded the point, the change was approved and the earlier approval retrospectively written into their records.

In 2010, the P&Ms became possibly the only British military unit to carry a third colour – the City Colour, reflecting its unique association with the City of London. The new colour was presented in 2010 at Ye Feast and shows the City arms – 'Argent a cross gules', in the 'upper hoist quadrant', a sword in pale point upwards. The presentation was slightly spoiled by that fact that the sword on the new colour was upside down, symbolising, in heraldic terms, dishonour, treason and death. The Keeper of Walbrook Hall, a senior officer at Mansion House, when asked to provide a suitable flag, remembered he had one in his cellar but was unaware that it had been placed there because of its faulty design; the fault was quickly rectified.

Later, when seeking permission to change from the late Queen's cypher to that of the King, it was thought prudent to seek confirmation of the Company's permission to carry the City's standard. Once again, calamity nearly struck, as it was found that authority to carry another's colours or flag rests with the sovereign on advice from the College of Arms, and it is generally deemed inappropriate for one body to carry the standard of another. Disaster was averted by the HAC Archivist, Justine Taylor, who located a purse at the British Museum dated 1693 which displayed the arms of the HAC and that of the City on either side. With this historic backing, the College felt it appropriate to allow the continued carrying of the City standard by the Company on the grounds of 'custom and usage'.

In March 2025, at a service in St Paul's, all three colours – Royal, P&M and City – were paraded down the nave and laid upon the altar under the rotunda. There they were blessed by the Dean of St Paul's in the three persons of the Trinity, as a sign of duty to King, Country and the City in the sight of God, ending with a request to God to:

> grant to all who follow these Standards your gracious favour
> in Jesus Christ our Lord.

Acknowledgements

Many people have helped to make this book possible. Particular thanks go to:

- Jon Baker, Roger Davenport, Tony Gabb, Rob Gillies, Tony O'Hagan, Rupert Pengelley, Hugh Tippett, Andrew Wallis and the P&M veterans' company for their comments and input
- Andrew Izod, Richard Ward and Paul Champness for their reminiscences
- Archivist Justine Taylor, for her continual support and inventiveness
- Richard Jackson, for commissioning me to write this book
- the P&M centenary committee, and above all, the indefatigable Serjeant Harbinger, Richard Peters, for their and his unfailing efforts and support.

I am grateful to those individuals and bodies who have given permission for illustrative material to be used, including The Company of Watermen and Lightermen, The Illustrated London News Limited, The London Transport Museum, The Standard Ltd, and Phil McCarthy Photography (philphotography@mac.com) [https://philmccarthyphotography.smugmug.com/Phil-McCarthy].

I am particularly grateful to Gerald Sharp Photography (www.sharpphoto.co.uk) and Peter Holland for permission to use some of the many photographs they have taken at Mansion House, Guildhall, The Lord Mayor's Show and other significant City events.

Every effort has been made to trace and acknowledge the copyright holders of the images used in this book. Where possible, permissions have been obtained for use, and appropriate credits have been provided. If you believe that any image has been used without proper acknowledgement or permission, please contact the publisher so that the omission can be rectified in future printings.

Sources and Further Reading

Original sources

Bamford Smith, J.: 13th Royal Fusiliers war diary and memoir.

Barriffe, Colonel: *Militarie Discipline or the Young Artillery-man* (6th edition, Gertrude Dawson, 1661).

Barriffe, William: *Mars, his triumph. Or, the description of an exercise performed the XVIII. of October, 1638, in Merchant-Taylors Hall by certain gentlemen of the Artillery Garden London* (John Legat 1639).

Champness, Geoffrey: memoir of a lift installation at Chartwell.

HAC archives.

HAC Journal.

HAC membership lists.

The Illustrated London News, The Graphic etc.

Lord Mayor's Show programmes.

Ministry of Information: *Roof over Britain* (War Office, 1943).

Pathé News online archives (https://www.britishpathe.com/).

P&M archives.

The Official Diary of Lieutenant-General Adam Williamson: Deputy-Lieutenant of the Tower of London 1722–1747 (Offices of the Society, 1912).

Ward, Laurence: *The London County Council Bomb Damage Maps 1939–1945* (Thames & Hudson, 2015).

Ward, Richard: *The Quartermaster's Tale* (privately circulated, 2018).

Secondary sources

Seventeenth century

Day, Jon: *Gloucester & Newbury 1643: The Turning Point of the Civil War* (Pen & Sword, 2007).

Emberton, Wilfred: *Skippon's Brave Boys: The origins, development and Civil War service of London's Trained Bands* (Barracuda Books, 1984).

Lawrence, David: *The Complete Soldier: Military Books and Military Culture in Early Stuart England 1603–1645* (Brill, 2009).

Roberts, Keith: *Pike and Shot Tactics 1590–1660* (Osprey, 2010).

Robertshaw, Andrew: 'Cavaliers on the Field of Mars: The Honourable Artillery company and London Trained Bands as the training ground for the officers of the "London Regiment"' in *A New Way of Fighting: Professionalism in the English Civil War*, ed. Serena Jones (Helion, 2017).
Scott, Chris and Turton, Alan: *Hey for Old Robin!: The Campaigns and Armies of the Earl of Essex During the First Civil War, 1642–44* (Helion, 2017).
Wanklyn, Malcolm and Jones, Frank: *A Military History of the English Civil War 1642-1649* (Routledge, 2005).

Second World War
Blake, Lewis: *Bromley in the Front Line* (Lewis Blake, 1980).
Churchill, Winston S.: *The Second World War Volume II: Their Finest Hour* (Cassell & Co., 1949).
Faith the cat: https://www.purr-n-fur.org.uk/famous/faith.html
Forczyk, Robert: *We March Against England: Operation Sea Lion, 1940–41* (Osprey, 2016).
Johnson, Brigadier R.F.: *Regimental Fire: The Honourable Aartillery Company in World War II* (William Lea, 1958).
Howgrave-Graham, H.M.: *The Metropolitan Police at War* (HMSO, 1947).
LDV: *The Bromley Home Guard: A History of the 51st Kent Battalion* (The Sun Engraving Co. Ltd, undated).
McKinstry, Leo: *Operation Sealion: How Britain Crushed the German War Machine's Dreams of Invasion in 1940* (John Murray, 2015).
Reeves, Graham: *Undaunted: The Story of Bromley in the Second World War* (Bromley Leisure Services, 1990).
Roof over Britain: The Official Story of the AA Defences 1939–1942 (HMSO, 1943).
White, Jerry: *The Battle of London 1939–45: Endurance, Heroism and Frailty Under Fire* (The Bodley Head, 2021).
Zeigler, Philip: *London at War* 1939–1945 (Pimlico, 2002).

General
Bartie, Angela et al. (eds.): *Restaging the Past: Historical Pageants, Culture and Society in Modern Britain* (UCL Press, 2020).
Binns, Lieut-Colonel P.L.: *The Story of the Royal Tournament* (Gale & Polden, 1952).
Cairncross, Sir Alec: *The British Economy Since 1945* (Blackwell, 1992).
Chalfont, Lord: *The Story of the Royal Tournament 1880–1980* (The Royal Tournament, 1980).
Edwards, Major T.L.: *Military Customs* (Gale & Polden, 1961).
Essex-Lopresti, Tim: *A Brief History of Civil Defence* (Civil Defence Association, 2005).

Girouard, Mark: *The Return to Camelot: Chivalry and the English Gentleman* (Yale University Press, 1981).

Goold Walker DSO, MC, G.: *The Honourable Artillery Company 1537–1987* (3rd edition, Honourable Artillery Company, 1986).

Greenglass, Graham: *Guildhall: City of London – History Guide Companion* (Pen & Sword, 2018).

Heath, Edward: *The Course of My Life* (Bloomsbury Reader, 2012).

Hope, Valerie: *My Lord Mayor* (Corporation of London, 1989).

Kynaston, David: *The City of London: Volume III Illusions of Gold 1914–1945* (Chatto & Windus, 1999).

Kynaston, David: *The City of London: Volume IV A Club No More 1945–2000* (Chatto & Windus, 2001).

Kynaston, David: *Austerity Britain 1945–51 (Tales of a New Jerusalem)* (Bloomsbury, 2007).

Marr, Andrew: *The History of Modern Britain* (Pan, 2017).

Owen, James: *Danger UXB: The Heroic Story of the WWII Bomb Disposal Teams* (Abacus, 2011).

Pevsner, Nikolaus: *The City of London (Pevsner Architectural Guides: Buildings of England)* (Yale University Press, 1997).

Withington, Robert: *English Pageantry: An Historical Outline*, Volume II, Chapter VI, 'The Lord Mayor's Show' (Harvard University Press, 1920).

Zeigler, Philip: *Edward Heath* (Harper Press, 2011).

Zweiniger-Bargielowska, Ina: *Austerity in Britain: Rationing, Controls, and Consumption, 1939–1955* (Oxford University Press, 2002).

Index